SECOND EDITION

Comprehension Strategies

for Middle Grade Learners

A HANDBOOK FOR
CONTENT AREA TEACHERS

Charlotte Rose Sadler

INTERNATIONAL
Reading Association
800 BARKSDALE ROAD, PO BOX 8139
NEWARK, DE 19714-8139, USA
www.reading.org

The International Reading Association attempts, through its publications, to provide a forum for a wide spectrum of opinions on reading. This policy permits divergent viewpoints without implying the endorsement of the Association.

Executive Editor, Publications   Shannon Fortner
Managing Editor   Christina M. Terranova
Editorial Associate   Wendy Logan
Design and Composition Manager   Anette Schuetz
Design and Composition Associate   Lisa Kochel

Cover   Design, Lise Holliker Dykes; Photographs (from top): © Creatas/Thinkstock, © Jupiterimages/Photos.com/Thinkstock, © EDHAR/Shutterstock Images

Library of Congress Cataloging-in-Publication Data

Sadler, Charlotte Rose, 1963-
  Comprehension strategies for middle grade learners : a handbook for content area teachers / Charlotte Rose Sadler. -- 2nd ed.
      p. cm.
  Includes bibliographical references.
  ISBN 978-0-87207-837-6
  1. Reading comprehension. 2. Reading (Middle school) I. International Reading Association. II. Title.

  LB1050.45.S33 2011
  428.4071'2--dc22

                    2011006565

Suggested APA Reference
Sadler, C.R. (2011). *Comprehension strategies for middle grade learners: A handbook for content area teachers* (2nd ed.). Newark, DE: International Reading Association.

This book is dedicated to the following people: My parents, Ray and Helen Rose, for their everlasting support of education throughout my life; my sister, Kathleen McKenzie, for giving input, reading revisions, and providing assistance and encouragement; my sister, Patricia Gerard, for providing inspiration; and my husband, Eric D. Sadler, who never questioned the numerous hours of work on this edition and for always being supportive.

Contents

SECTION THREE
Connecting to Previous Knowledge   57

SECTION FOUR
Improving Organization   87

SECTION FIVE
Promoting Independent Learning

SECTION SIX
Teaching to Learning Style

About the Author

Charlotte Rose Sadler is first and foremost an educator of students and a supporter of teachers. She is the principal of Parsons Elementary School in Gwinnett County Public Schools in Suwanee, Georgia, USA. As the focus of the schools and school system is teaching and learning—with an emphasis on learning—she focuses on providing support to teachers in order to allow them to help students succeed academically and become lifelong learners.

Charlotte received her bachelor's degree in music education from Berry College in Rome, Georgia, and her master's degree in middle grades from Brenau University in Gainesville, Georgia. She received her reading specialist certification while teaching students in grades 4–7, and then served as a middle school reading specialist. Her doctorate in educational leadership is from the University of Georgia in Athens, where her work centered on legal rights and responsibilities of public school educators. She served as an assistant principal for six years prior to becoming a principal.

Charlotte's first edition of *Comprehension Strategies for Middle Grade Learners: A Handbook for Content Area Teachers* was well received as a tool for teachers at various levels. Her second edition includes additional strategies and addresses technology and its uses in reading comprehension. She has also contributed a chapter entitled "Reading Comprehension Strategies for Struggling Middle School Learners" to *Teaching African American Learners to Read: Perspectives and Practices* (International Reading Association, 2005).

When not working at school, Charlotte enjoys spending time with her husband, Eric, and their numerous cats, including their Siamese mix, Maile. Her hobbies include reading, writing, drawing, doing home-improvement projects, and collecting cat-themed items.

Introduction

This second edition of *Comprehension Strategies for Middle Grade Learners: A Handbook for Content Area Teachers* includes 21 new strategies to assist middle grade learners in the content areas. These strategies were added to expand the usefulness of the text and incorporate strategies that have been developed since the first edition. All of the original strategies have been retained for their continued usefulness. The combination of original and new strategies will allow readers to have a broader variety of strategies from which to select. Because of overwhelming responses from readers who appreciated the simplified and easy-to-read layout of the original edition, the format of the second edition has not been altered substantially. A reflection section has been added to each strategy, which provides questions for readers to consider what did and did not work and how the strategy can be improved in the future. An appendix has been added that addresses the use of technology with comprehension strategies, as its uses and implications have increased in the past decade.

As educators, we strive to prepare students to become successful, contributing members of society. Reading is a vital part of this preparedness. It is more than matching sounds with letters or learning sight words. Reading involves comprehension—understanding what is read, what is meant, what is implied. When students have comprehension difficulties, the task of text instruction becomes increasingly complicated for educators. How can students learn from text if they cannot understand their assigned readings? This issue can be approached from different perspectives depending on the grade level of the students.

For teachers of middle school students, there are two issues to consider. First, many of the texts students encounter in middle school are informational, which differ in organization and structure from the fiction and poetry students encounter in the elementary grades. It is important to identify these differences and determine how best to help students in comprehending a variety of texts (Blachowicz & Ogle, 2001). The focus on reading a variety of texts for a variety of purposes is also evident in the Common Core State Standards (2010), which have been adopted by the majority of states in the United States. The purpose of this initiative is to ensure that parents, students, and teachers know what learning is expected of students to achieve college and career readiness. The reading standards encourage students to read a variety of classic and contemporary literature as well as a variety of informational texts.

Second, by the time students have reached middle school, they are expected to read and comprehend grade-level texts. Many middle school teachers are uncertain how to approach instructing students who have difficulties with text comprehension. They may assume that this is the job of the reading teacher, or they may feel they do not have the skills to teach reading. However, according to Radcliffe, Caverly, Hand, and Franke (2008), every teacher should have the necessary knowledge and skills to integrate reading throughout the content areas. Comprehension must be *taught* [my emphasis]. It is the essence of reading and cannot be left to chance (Opitz & Eldridge, 2004). In reality, we are all reading teachers. If students have a problem reading or comprehending the text we have assigned, it is our job to assist them. Once we have an understanding of this, it is important to have the necessary tools to teach both reading and content (Massey & Heafner, 2004). Strategies, such as the ones provided in this book, are designed to assist both the teacher with instructing and the student with comprehending and learning. The strategies are useful with a diverse range of students, including English learners.

In addition to assisting students with strategies for comprehension, we must also provide them with the skills to use these strategies independently as they encounter even more complex texts in high school and postsecondary education. We are constantly building background knowledge, and reading to learn is a lifelong process (Marcell, DeCleene, & Juettner, 2010). Researchers and literacy specialists agree that learning to read does not end in the elementary schools. As students move into middle and high schools, reading becomes more complex; therefore, teachers at these levels need strategies to help students comprehend more sophisticated texts (Tovani, 2004). The Common Core State Standards reinforce the importance of text complexity, giving equal weight to the sophistication of what students read and the skill with which they read. The reading standards specifically offer a staircase of increasing text complexity, thereby ensuring preparation for college- and career-level reading. Reading comprehension is a process that takes place over time and is about finding meaning in text. It is our responsibility to ensure that students are provided with the necessary instruction to comprehend and analyze what has been read and to move students toward independence in reading comprehension (Au, 2009).

This book offers 77 strategies with descriptions, discussions, and examples of how they can be used in different content areas. Included with each strategy are a description and its purpose, content area examples, assessment suggestions, and reflection questions. Depending on the student reading differences in the classroom, these strategies can be used with individuals, small groups, or the entire class.

The strategies have been divided into six sections based on their primary goal. Section One, Checking for Understanding, features strategies that will assist you in assessing the level of students' comprehension and show you how to help students increase their comprehension. Section Two, Fostering Cooperative Learning, contains strategies that will help students work cooperatively—a skill that is necessary in many jobs—and increase their comprehension through peer support. Section Three, Connecting to Previous Knowledge, provides strategies that allow students to connect the information they are reading to knowledge or interests they already have. These strategies are especially useful in motivating students and creating interest in new topics. Section Four, Improving Organization, provides strategies for helping students organize material in a way that will improve their comprehension. These strategies incorporate the use of outlines, charts, and graphic organizers. Section Five, Promoting Independent Learning, offers strategies that students can learn and apply independently in numerous situations. These strategies provide students with a way to approach a particular concept, word, or section of text, or to question and break down the information into steps to increase their levels of understanding. Section Six, Teaching to Learning Style, contains strategies that focus on one or more modes of learning (e.g., visual, auditory, tactile). Because students learn in a variety of ways, you can use these strategies to help students with particular learning styles who have strength in a certain modality. The Appendix, Technology and Comprehension, addresses technology and its possible uses for reading comprehension. It offers brief descriptions of technology and technology-related resources as well as ideas for how each may be used to assist with comprehension in the content areas.

The strategies presented in this collection are not comprehensive, but they will enhance students' learning experiences through a variety of modes and methods that may encourage the reluctant reader and enrich the experience of the enthusiastic reader. This variety gives students the opportunity to gain comprehension through the mode or strategy that best suits them individually. It is my desire that students discover a variety of strategies that will assist them in comprehension that they can use independently as lifelong learners.

Checking for Understanding

This section features strategies that assist you in assessing the level of students' comprehension and show how to help students increase their comprehension. Awareness of comprehension level is important to you and to the students in your classroom. It is best when you are able to check for understanding at many times during a lesson or unit to see if you need to go back over information or clarify a misunderstanding. Checking at the conclusion of a lesson is also vital. Many of the strategies in this section require students to share the information they have learned with you or with another student. The student is able to use these strategies to assess the information he or she has comprehended in a format that is not strictly reading questions and writing out answers.

Click and Clunk

LANGUAGE ARTS

SOCIAL STUDIES

SCIENCE

MATH

Click and Clunk is an excellent means to assess what information the students have learned and what information needs to be covered in more depth. This strategy helps students recognize the information they do not understand and assists them in getting the information they need. It motivates students as they attempt to increase the information they understand (clicks) and decrease what they do not understand (clunks).

Procedure

Have students create two columns on their paper and label them "Click" and "Clunk." Next, have the students read a passage, then list what they really understand (click) and what they do not understand (clunk). As a group, discuss the clunks and try to clarify the information. This can be done through instructing students directly or by allowing students who understand the issue to explain it to the class.

Language Arts
Topic: Parts of Speech

Click	Clunk
nouns	adverbs
verbs	prepositions
adjectives	interjections
pronouns	

Social Studies
Topic: Roman Republic

Click	Clunk
dictator	plebeian
republic	patrician
veto	consul
why it collapsed	why a republic was formed

Science
Topic: Solutions and Physical Science

Click	Clunk
concentrated	saturated
matter	diluted
colloid	
solvent	

Math
Topic: Equations and Inequalities

Click	Clunk
solving equations	polynomials
operations	function notation
variables	

Assessment

After covering the material, ensure that students chose clunk words that assisted in comprehension. Discuss the Click–Clunk list again to see if all the clunk terms can be changed to click terms. Those terms in the "Clunk" column that are clearly understood can be moved to the "Click" column, and any terms remaining in the "Clunk" column should be explained further.

Vaughn & Klingner, 1999

(continued)

Reflection

- How could you guide students to ensure they know all of the necessary vocabulary for comprehension?
- How could you assist students who were unable to determine which words would help them in comprehending the material?
- Was the text appropriate for this strategy?
- Did students have the necessary vocabulary to comprehend the selection?
- Was there an appropriate balance between teacher-led discussion and student-led discussion?
- Did students choose clunk works that could have been figured out by using context?
- What could you have done differently to make this activity more successful?
- What worked well?

Cued Retelling

Cued retelling is when a partner helps to prompt with retelling of a story. Having a prepared list of important information helps students recognize those things they should cover. After time, students may be able to generate their own lists of items that should be covered during a retelling.

Procedure

Prepare a list of important information that you would like the students to know. Have students read the story or text independently, then have students work with a partner and retell the information they have just read. The student who is listening should have a copy of the information you would like known to ensure that all points have been mentioned.

Language Arts
- Read a story dealing with animals or human experiences. Students seem to be able to relate to these topics, which makes retelling easier.
- Distribute a sheet for summarizing/cues (e.g., character description, motivation, plot, setting, main topic, vocabulary).
- Pair students and ask them to follow procedures.

Social Studies
- Read a section of text on Egypt.
- Distribute sheet for summarizing/cues (e.g., how Egyptians lived, their religion, the climate, pharaohs, gods).
- Pair students and ask them to follow procedures.

Assessment

Use your teacher questioning, observation of retelling, worksheets, or quizzes to determine comprehension. Students should be able to correctly retell the story or text. If they are unable to do so, they should reread the text (possibly aloud with a partner), then attempt the paired procedure again. Students who are still having difficulties should try this strategy with a shorter or simpler text selection.

Reflection

- Was your prepared list adequate to provide comprehension?
- What are ways students could assess the retelling other than with a prepared list?
- How could you prepare students to use this strategy independently?
- What could you have done differently to make this activity more successful?
- What worked well?

D. Mancus (personal communication, September 2000); Vaughn & Klingner, 1999

LANGUAGE ARTS

SOCIAL STUDIES

SCIENCE

Discussion

Although this seems like a basic and simple strategy, the depth and level of discussion can contribute to comprehension and can incorporate other skills, such as communication and organization. With Discussion, students attend to vocabulary as they come to it instead of prior to reading the selection. This strategy allows you to check for understanding by providing immediate feedback from the students rather than waiting for written feedback. If students are having difficulty understanding the selection, you may need to supply additional information to increase the students' level of understanding.

Procedure

Begin by reading a selection aloud or independently. The class should then discuss what is important in the particular piece, such as character motivation. Encourage students to voice their opinions and support their viewpoints.

Language Arts
Discuss the motivation of the characters and why they do what they do. Read "Your Three Minutes Are Up" by Ellen Conford and ask, Do you think Libby's father is being fair? Why does Libby feel as she does? What does *inalienable* mean? How did Libby's point of view change after Mark's call?

Social Studies
Discuss Africa's first people and ask, How did early Africans get their food? What civilizations arose along the Nile River? What do you know about Ancient Egypt? What are some achievements of ancient Egyptian and Nubian civilizations?

Science
Discuss the nature of light and ask, What is reflection? How does light travel? What material does light move through the fastest? What are the differences among opaque, transparent, and translucent?

Assessment

Through observation and questioning during the discussion, determine students' level of comprehension. Refer to the text as needed to support the discussion.

Alvermann et al., 1996

Reflection

- How effective was this strategy with your students?
- How could you transfer question generation from yourself to your students?
- Were students able to support their viewpoints?
- How much guidance did you need to provide throughout the discussion?
- What could you have done differently to make this activity more successful?
- What worked well?

DRAW

DRAW stands for *Draw*, *Read*, *Attend*, and *Write*. This strategy involves reading, writing, speaking, and listening. It encourages higher order thinking, motivates students in gaining information, promotes discussion, encourages listening, and promotes participation. The level of the questions that are chosen is important.

Procedure

Students are given a selection to read. You prepare several questions that address various levels of comprehension. These questions are numbered and should be placed in an order that helps to encourage discussion. Students are given sheets with all the questions. You cut one sheet so that each question is on a strip. The strips are mixed, and students *draw* strips. Next, students *read* the selection.

Students are responsible for answering the question they have chosen, but they must read all of the selection in order to be able to answer a quiz at the end. Once everyone has read the selection, you call for responses to questions, starting with the first question. Throughout the responses to the questions, encourage discussion by asking leading questions to allow students to demonstrate their understanding.

Students must *attend* to the answers. Once all questions have been answered, students put up their question sheets and strips. You read each question aloud, and students *write* the answers. The selection of questions is most important. They should include some which are literal and some which require inference. The quiz provides a purpose for students and provides a means of assessment for you.

Language Arts
Topic: *The Story of My Life* by Helen Keller
- How did the arrival of a teacher affect Helen's life?
- What kind of person do you think Helen Keller was as a young girl? (Consider the challenges she faced.)
- If Helen were a child today, how might her life be different?

Social Studies
Topic: Asia—India
- What is the primary religion in India?
- How do monsoons affect India's culture?
- What challenges are caused by India's caste system?

Agnew, 2000

Science
Topic: Fossils
- How does a petrified fossil form?
- Which organism has a better chance of becoming a fossil: a jellyfish or a bony fish? Explain.
- Describe the process for forming a fossil.
- Fossil seashells have been found on land. What can you infer from this?

Math
Topic: Volume of Prisms and Cylinders
- What is volume?
- How can you use the length, width, and height of a prism to find the total number of cubes without counting them?
- When the height of a cylinder is doubled, how does the volume change?

Assessment

After giving the quiz, determine the students' level of understanding by assessing their responses. If needed, have students revisit the text. Students should be able to answer questions, both literal and inferential. If students are unable to do so, it would be beneficial to either work individually with the student (or group of students) or partner the student with another student to model locating answers to the questions in the text.

Reflection

- Did your students demonstrate understanding of the text?
- Were the questions chosen varied enough to encourage both recall and higher order thinking?
- What other leading questions might you offer to promote discussion?
- What could you have done differently to make this activity more successful?
- What worked well?

Games

After covering the set material for a particular unit in a subject, use games as instructional tools to review the information and to check for understanding. Students tend to enjoy this strategy and learn more than if they were taking notes and answering questions. They are more motivated and involved in their learning.

Procedure

Games can be as simple as dividing the class into teams and asking questions, awarding points for correct answers. You may choose to use a "Jeopardy" format with more structured information presented on the board. Another popular format is "Who Wants to Be a Millionaire." Use a quick, initial round and three simple rounds before declaring a winner and beginning again.

Language Arts
"Who Wants to Be a Millionaire" Format

Question	Answers			
Who was the main character?	A. Libby	B. Stacey	C. Mother	D. Mark
In the story, Libby was	A. selfish	B. jealous	C. sensitive	D. quiet

Social Studies
"Jeopardy" Format

Question	Answer
The average weather of a place over several years	What is climate?
The total number of people in a given area	What is population?

Science
"Jeopardy" Format

Question	Answer
The three states of matter	What are solid, liquid, gas?
The stages of metamorphosis of a butterfly	What are egg, larva, pupa, adult?

Math
Read word problems and have short-answer competitions with simple problem solving. The first group with a correct answer gets 5 points; all groups that get a correct answer get 3 points.

Bean & Zigmond, 1994

Assessment

Evaluate answers to determine comprehension. If one team is unable to answer a question, allow another team an attempt to answer. If no one can answer the question correctly, share the answer with the students and use the same question at a later time.

Reflection

- What popular games could you adapt to use in the classroom?
- How could you adapt this strategy to be used in centers or groups?
- How could you best guide students in the creation of questions?
- What could you have done differently to make this activity more successful?
- What worked well?

Get the Gist

This strategy helps students to focus on the main idea in a passage. It also gives them the opportunity to learn how others think as they state their ideas and reasons. This allows you to check students' understanding of summarization and to determine if they can correctly identify the main idea.

Procedure

Have the students read a short passage, then discuss with them what the passage was about. Ask individual students to identify if the passage was mainly about a person, place, or thing, and decide what was most important. Ask the class members if they agree. If they do not, have others explain what they feel was most important. After discussion, have each student write one sentence summarizing what the class decided was the main idea. Begin with short passages or simple concepts before moving students toward longer passages and more complex ideas.

Language Arts
Topic: Adjectives as a part of speech
Passage about: thing (words)
Summarizing sentence: Adjectives are words that are used to describe nouns.
(This activity can be done with stories, but limit it to a couple of paragraphs at a time.)

Social Studies
Topic: Rome's beginnings
Passage about: people
Summarizing sentence: We do not know a great deal about the original founders of Rome; however, we know that they used many ideas from the people they defeated, such as the Greeks.

Science
Topic: Glacier
Passage about: thing
Summarizing sentence: Glaciers are huge masses of moving snow and ice that change the land by scraping, deposition, and erosion.

Assessment

Evaluate the summary sentence to determine if students were able to state the main idea.

Swanson & De La Paz, 1998; Vaughn & Klingner, 1999

Reflection

- Were your students able to get the main idea without prompting from you?
- How could you assist students who were unable to identify the main idea?
- What changes could you make to provide additional support to struggling students?
- What could you have done differently to make this activity more successful?
- What worked well?

Interactive Read-Alouds

This strategy involves reading text aloud and posing questions throughout the reading to involve students in the learning process. Through guided questions, students are able to share their knowledge with one another. This is an uncomplicated means of determining students' level of understanding because no materials are necessary and you can receive immediate feedback.

Procedure

To be effective, be prepared with planned questions to stimulate discussion. It is also important to anticipate when it may be necessary to build background knowledge for the students. Read a text aloud and pose questions throughout the reading. Invite brief interactions with the students, who may respond personally or interpersonally.

Language Arts

Read a few paragraphs in a story, then ask topic-specific questions such as What can you tell me about the main character at this time? What is the main idea of this passage?

Social Studies

Read about climate and vegetation in the desert. Ask questions such as What makes a cactus able to survive in the desert? What causes an oasis to exist?

Science

Read about prisms and ask questions such as What causes the colors to form as light passes through a prism? How is this related to a rainbow?

Math

Read word problems, then ask questions such as What is the problem asking you to do? Which operations do you need to use? How should you set up this problem?

Assessment

Use your teacher observations, discussion, and correct responses to questions to determine comprehension. Your observations should include monitoring the involvement of individual students and their responses. Discussion can be used to determine students' level of comprehension by assessing their responses. Encourage responses from students who appear off task. If students do not respond correctly, provide additional information and refer to the text to reexamine the passage.

Barrentine, 1996

Reflection

- Did you have questions that stimulated discussion and included higher order thinking?
- Was there real interaction with the text, you, and your students?
- How could you help students to relate the passage to their own lives?
- What could you have done differently to make this activity more successful?
- What worked well?

Narrative Pyramid

Narrative Pyramid allows the reader to summarize and make connections. This is also an excellent strategy to help students organize their writing. This strategy is used after reading a story. It is best to do this first as a class. After time, students should be able to generate their own narrative pyramids.

Procedure

Have students read the selection. Show students the format for writing a narrative pyramid.

- Line 1—character name
- Line 2—two descriptive words for character
- Line 3—three words describing setting
- Line 4—four words describing the problem
- Line 5—five words describing an event
- Line 6—six words describing another event
- Line 7—seven words describing another event
- Line 8—eight words describing the solution to the problem

Create the narrative pyramid, and use it as a basis for discussion involving the whole class. Prompt students as necessary.

Language Arts
"Casey at the Bat" by Ernest Lawrence Thayer

Casey
Baseball player
Mudville baseball game
Mudville team is behind
Two struck out in ninth
Casey was very sure of himself
Casey let two strikes fly past him
Casey swung, struck out, and Mudville team lost

Assessment

Use your teacher questioning, observation of lines in the pyramid, and discussion to determine comprehension. Refer to the text as needed to support the discussion. Ensure the narrative pyramids gave an overall summary of the text so someone

Jonson, 2006; McLaughlin & Allen, 2009; Waldo, 1991

unfamiliar with the poem would be able to read the pyramids and have an understanding of the original text.

Reflection

- How could you assist students who have difficulties identifying the problem and solution?
- How could you assist students who have difficulties limiting each line to the specific number of words?
- How important is the number of words to the strategy?
- What could you have done differently to make this activity more successful?
- What worked well?

Page and Paragraph

This strategy assists you in checking for understanding by allowing students to respond to questions after reading short passages. It helps students to get started with reading a section and allows them to see how larger sections of text can be broken down into smaller parts. This is generally used as a start-up strategy to help the entire class begin to focus on the text.

Procedure

Begin by reading aloud a portion of the selection. Then allow students to read silently. Students who have difficulties comprehending while reading silently may continue oral reading in a small group without disrupting the entire class.

Language Arts

Read the first page of a story aloud. Have students read a specified amount silently. Stop and assess comprehension through discussion and questions. Repeat the process throughout the story and allow students who need to read aloud to continue to do so in small groups.

Social Studies/Science

Choose a text. Read one paragraph aloud in the first section. Allow students to finish the section silently. Walk around and assess. Allow those who need to continue reading aloud to do so.

Assessment

Monitor the involvement of individual students and their responses. Discussion can be used to determine students' level of comprehension by assessing their responses after reading. You should encourage responses from students who appear off task. Students should correctly respond to questions during a discussion or quiz. Assist students who need to continue to read aloud by pairing them with other readers.

Reflection

- Did you monitor enough to know that all the students were comprehending?
- Should you have prompted more discussion?
- What could you have done differently to make this activity more successful?
- What worked well?

J. Pederson (personal communication, September, 2000)

Paraphrasing/Summarizing

This strategy involves reading a paragraph or short section, putting the information aside, asking questions about the main idea and important details, then putting the main idea and details into your own words in complete sentences. This is a strategy that is necessary not only for comprehension, but also for reports and term papers. It assesses students' comprehension because they cannot rely on the author's wording.

Procedure

Model this strategy before the students attempt it. Follow these steps:

1. Explain to students the skills of paraphrasing and summarizing.

2. Model summarizing short passages.

3. Give students guided practice.

4. Have the students individually practice paraphrasing with brief segments then move to larger passages for summarizing. Check to ensure understanding.

5. Extend the concept and have students use it on their own.

Students should be encouraged to make their summaries informative yet brief. Use a portion of text that has already been studied, before trying it with unfamiliar text.

Language Arts
Read: *The men labored day after day preparing for the flood. There were numerous times when they would work for 16 hours without a break.*
Own words: The men worked for days—often for 16 hours without a break—as they prepared for the flood.

Social Studies
Read: *All the streams and rivers in a major drainage basin form a river system. The Mississippi River system drains about one third of the United States.*
Own words: The Mississippi River is a major river system, consisting of numerous streams and rivers, that drains approximately one third of the United States.

Science
Read: *The electricity supplied by a battery flows in one direction. This is called a direct current.*
Own words: A direct current is when electricity flows in one direction—like in a battery.

(continued)

Gunning, 1996; Katims & Harris, 1997; Vacca & Vacca, 1989

Assessment

Determine comprehension through discussion and evaluation of paraphrased statements. Discussion can be used to determine students' level of comprehension by assessing their responses after reading. Encourage responses from students who appear off task. Students should correctly respond to questions during a discussion. Evaluate the paraphrased statements and determine if the students have correctly summarized the passage. If students have difficulties with this, have other students share their paraphrasing or model paraphrasing to assist them.

Reflection

- How could you ensure that your students understand the skill and importance of paraphrasing?
- Do students understand the importance of paraphrasing?
- Do students understand the differences between paraphrasing and summarizing?
- How could you assist students whose summaries did not show comprehension of the passage?
- What could you have done differently to make this activity more successful?
- What worked well?

Problem of the Week

This strategy is especially useful in mathematics but can also be used in grammar to gain insight into the thought process that students use in their problem solving. Because this is done each week, it is easier to determine the progress of the students and to decide what additional problem-solving strategies may need to be taught.

Procedure

Each week, place or write a problem on the chalkboard. Give students these specific steps to follow:

1. Restate the problem in students' own words.
2. Describe the procedure they used (who helped and what was tried).
3. Describe what was learned and if the concept had been seen before.
4. Give the answer; determine if it is reasonable and if there is more than one possible answer.
5. Make certain at least two adults or peers have proofread the paper before it is turned in.

Language Arts

Write: *She was disgusted I really hate it Mary said when we don't have any money therefore I think we should wait until we save our allowance before we go out*
Have students state what needs to be done with punctuation. Discuss why each type of punctuation is used.

Math

Word problem: Four seventh graders went to the movies. Mary had $7, Ben had $11, Jen had $6, and Lynn had $12. Tickets cost $3.50 each. Each person bought a soda for $1.00, popcorn for $.75, and a candy bar for $.50. Ben bought two posters for $3.00 each. How much money was spent? How much money does each person have left? What is the total amount left? If the amount left were divided equally, how much would each person get?

Assessment

Evaluate the final answer to determine if it is correct and if it gives a reasonable explanation for solving the problem.

(continued)

Fuentes, 1998

Reflection

- Did you choose a problem that would adequately challenge your students?
- How could you incorporate this into a cooperative group or peer activity?
- Would this strategy be useful if done more often than once a week?
- What could you have done differently to make this activity more successful?
- What worked well?

Questions Into Paragraphs (QuIP)

QuIP is a strategy that provides a framework to initiate research and structure writing. It allows students to focus on a particular question or set of questions and extract information that assists in overall comprehension of the material. This strategy is best used with informational text.

Procedure

Assign or have students choose a topic to explore. Show the layout of the QuIP grid and have them write their topic at the top. Have students come up with three questions related to their topic and write them in the grid. Students should choose two sources to research their questions. These may be student selected or from a list of sources you have approved—depending on the topic and reading ability of the student. As students research, they record answers in the grid. After the grid has been completed, students write an informational paragraph that they share with a partner or in a small group.

Language Arts
Topic: Plot

Question	Source A (textbook)	Source B (Internet)
What are the parts of a plot?	conflict, rising action, climax, outcome	exposition, rising action, climax, falling action, resolution

Paragraph:
  The plot of a story has a variety of parts. There is generally a conflict presented at the beginning, followed by rising action to keep the interest of the reader. The action peaks with a climax. This is followed by falling action that leads to the outcome or resolution.

Social Studies
Topic: Soil Conservation

Question	Source A (textbook)	Source B (Internet)
What are ways to manage soil conservation?	Contour plowing Conservation plowing Leave soil to lie fallow Crop rotation	Gardening Keep soil moist Keep vegetation strong and healthy Find suitable tillage method Add physical structures Build wind barrier Plant patches of high grass Create organic mulch Plant vegetation that assists Water plants in early morning

(continued)

McLaughlin, 1987; McLaughlin & Allen, 2009; Waldo, 1991

Paragraph:
    As we seek to be more responsible to the environment, soil conservation is important. There are many ways to manage soil conservation. Crop rotation or leaving the soil to lie fallow can allow the soil to recover. Contour plowing or finding the appropriate tillage method is also important. Providing a wind barrier and planting specific vegetation can assist in less erosion. It is also best to water plants in the early morning hours. All of these are ways to manage soil conservation.

Science

Topic: Animal Behaviors

Questions	Source A (textbook)	Source B (Internet)
What are the functions of most of an animal's behaviors?	Help an animal survive or reproduce	Find and defend resources Avoid predators Choose mates and reproduce Care for young

Paragraph:
    As we study animals, we are able to determine that many of their behaviors have specific functions. Some of their behaviors help them to choose mates, reproduce, and protect their young. Other behaviors may assist them in avoiding predators, finding resources, and surviving. We can determine the function of many of these behaviors through observation and research.

Assessment

Review student paragraphs to determine comprehension. The paragraphs should provide adequate details and a summary in order to show the text covered is understood. Main ideas should be evident. If student comprehension is not evident, they should reread the text (possibly with a partner) and discuss. This strategy can be used with a partner or group or as a whole-group activity.

Reflection

- Did students have difficulty in developing three questions?
- What assistance might you offer next time to assist students in developing their questions?
- Were students able to locate answers to their questions?
- Did students use a variety of questions?
- Did the student paragraphs demonstrate full comprehension of the text?
- Did the chosen sources adequately provide information for the paragraph?
- What could you have done differently to make this activity more successful?
- What worked well?

Retelling

Retelling is powerful because it requires a deep understanding of a passage. This strategy is more detailed than summarizing in that it asks students to tell what the story or text is about by using their own words. The text cannot be summed up in a few sentences. Students must be aware of details and sequence. This strategy can be used with an entire class, but there will be more participation with the use of partners.

Procedure

Introduce what retelling is and give an example. Explain that retelling focuses only on the main elements. (In fiction, the main elements include story problem, main plot, resolution of the problem, and ending. In nonfiction, the main elements include main idea, details, sequential presentation, and description.) Give guided practice using a story that has already been read. Students should be allowed to work in pairs to read and retell the passages. Students may find it helpful to use note cards to list and organize the elements before retelling.

Language Arts

Use this activity with stories, poems, or grammar rules. Students read and tell the main points to their partner. The partner may use the book to see if everything important has been covered.

Social Studies/Science

Use with short text selections. Have students alternate retelling sections throughout a chapter. The partner can prompt for additional information.

Assessment

Observe during paired retellings, discussion, and a quiz or test to determine comprehension. Your observation should include monitoring the involvement of individual students during the paired retelling. Discussion helps determine students' comprehension level by assessing their responses after reading. Encourage responses from students who appear off task. Students should correctly respond to questions during a discussion or quiz. If students do not respond correctly, have their partners assist them and refer back to the text.

Reflection

- How could you ensure that your students retell the important aspects of the text?
- What should the partners be doing while the other student is doing the retelling?
- Would prompting assist students?
- What could you have done differently to make this activity more successful?
- What worked well?

Gunning, 1996

Fostering Cooperative Learning

This section contains strategies that are designed to improve the comprehension of students through working with partners or small groups. Not all students work best on their own, and these strategies allow for those students to look to their classmates. These strategies are especially useful in situations in which you believe a student can increase his or her comprehension with peer support. We live in a socially interactive society, and many students enjoy social networking and interacting with others. Being able to work cooperatively is a skill that is necessary in many jobs or careers. The strategies in this section can be used with small groups or with an entire class.

Circle-Seat-Center

LANGUAGE ARTS

SOCIAL STUDIES

SCIENCE

This strategy allows students to work in small peer groups and go over all the information you would like to cover. The strategy can reinforce information in a variety of ways: The Circle group focuses on verbal learning, the Seat group focuses on visual learning, and the Center group focuses on tactile learning. This also allows students who learn through different modalities the opportunity to learn through their strengths.

Procedure

First, instruct students to read the text. Following this, divide the class into three groups based on instructional needs. Give each group an assignment: Circle, Seat, or Center. The Circle group covers information in the text with your assistance. The Seat group members work individually or within their group to go over the text using worksheets and study sheets. The Center group works on projects, individually or in the group, related to the text. After a designated amount of time, students rotate to another group.

Language Arts
Topic: Parts of Speech
Circle: Discuss and clarify the topic.
Seat: Students identify the parts of speech using worksheets or skills sheets.
Center: Students create cards to be used in a game.

Social Studies
Topic: Fall of Rome
Circle: Discuss text, including reasons for the fall of Rome.
Seat: Students respond to questions and complete worksheets.
Center: Students create a timeline of the Roman Empire.

Science
Topic: Matter in Solution
Circle: Discuss the types of solutions.
Seat: Students complete worksheets or respond to questions at end of section.
Center: Students create charts to classify types of solutions.

Assessment

Evaluate using student participation and your teacher observation of information covered during discussion, correct answers on worksheets, and evaluation of information covered in projects to determine students' level of comprehension.

Ivey, 1999b

(continued)

Reflection

- Were students placed in the appropriate groups for the given assignment?
- Were all students actively engaged as well as equally engaged (within each group)?
- What could you have done differently to make this activity more successful?
- What worked well?

Classwide Peer Tutoring

LANGUAGE ARTS

SOCIAL STUDIES

SCIENCE

MATH

This strategy enables students to learn from their peers and requires 30 to 45 minutes of class time. This strategy is helpful because it allows students to share understanding of the text in a nonthreatening manner with their peers.

Procedure

First, pair students. (This pairing should change each time this strategy is used.) During the first 10 minutes, one student (tutor) assists the other student (tutee) with content information from a specific unit or subject area, presented orally, visually, or both. For the next 5 to 10 minutes, the tutor assesses the tutee's learning by having the tutee restate the information orally and in writing. The tutor gives 2 points to the tutee for each correct piece of information. If the tutor has to assist the tutee, the tutee gets 1 point when the information is given correctly.

The object is to go over as much information as possible and gain as many points as possible. Next, the pair should switch roles and repeat the process. At the end of class, check the points scored for each individual. The students may need to practice this strategy a few times before they are comfortable with it. As they become familiar with the strategy, the level of success should increase.

Language Arts
Discuss concepts in grammar and usage, rules, vocabulary, and information in a story.

Social Studies
Discuss various topics related to life in Ancient Greece, such as "in the marketplace," "at home," "slavery," and "women." Have specific information you would like the student to know pertaining to each topic.

Science
Discuss structure, functions, and parts of a plant; life cycle of a moss; structure/function of a flower; methods of seed dispersal; and role of stomata in gas exchange. Compare and contrast vascular and nonvascular, plants that produce seeds in cones and those in plants, and photosynthesis and respiration.

Math
Discuss and explain concepts such as ratio, proportion, percent, area, volume, and equations.

Arreaga-Mayer, 1998; Delquadri, Greenwood, Stretton, & Hall, 1983

(continued)

Assessment

Use evaluation of points earned, discussion, your teacher questioning, and a quiz or test to determine comprehension. A worksheet can be created with specific information to be covered and specific points assigned to assist the tutor. Monitor the involvement of individual students and their responses. Discussion can be used to determine students' level of comprehension by assessing their responses after reading. Encourage responses from students who appear off task. Students should correctly respond to questions in a discussion, on a quiz, or on a worksheet. Allow students who do not respond correctly to spend additional time working with their partner in going over the information.

Reflection

- How could you best pair students for this activity?
- After students switch roles, how do their scores compare?
- Is this consistent across the class?
- What other extending activities could you offer for those students who need more challenging material?
- What support could you offer to students who continue to struggle?
- What could you have done differently to make this activity more successful?
- What worked well?

Fishbowl

LANGUAGE ARTS

SOCIAL STUDIES

SCIENCE

Fishbowl is a strategy that promotes discussion among students about a text they have read. Students ask questions they have prepared, answer other students' questions, and debate issues. It is important for students to listen and attend to the questions and discussion in order to participate and show understanding following the activity.

Procedure

After reading a text you have selected, students are instructed to develop a list of three or four questions. The room is set up where there is an inner circle with seven chairs and an outer circle with enough chairs to seat the remainder of the class. Five students are selected as panelists to be in the inner circle while the two remaining chairs are left unoccupied. These are "jump seats" for other students who want to enter the discussion and then return to the audience.

Students in the outer circle take notes on the comments made by students in the inner circle, and only students in the inner circle may speak. Students in the inner circle take turns asking questions, giving answers, and discussing. After a designated amount of time, students in the fishbowl summarize their discussion. You guide students as needed until they are able to use this strategy independently. Throughout the strategy, you should note the discussion, student participation, and level of comprehension demonstrated.

Language Arts
Topic: *The Story of My Life* by Helen Keller
Questions: How did the arrival of a teacher change Helen's life? What might her life have been like without a teacher?
Discussion: How would our life be different if we faced the same challenges as Helen? What impact does a teacher have on our lives? Overall, what impact did the teacher have on Helen?

Social Studies
Topic: India and the Caste System
Questions: What impact do monsoons have on India's culture? What problems are created by the caste system?
Discussion: What would be different if India did not have monsoons? Do we have a system like the caste system? What influences in India affect its culture and how do they do this?

Science
Topic: Fossils
Questions: How do we know if fossils are real? What organisms leave the best fossils and why?
Discussion: Could fossils be faked? What does a fossil tell us about our past?

Jonson, 2006

(continued)

Assessment

Use your teacher observation throughout the questions, answers, and discussions to determine students' level of comprehension. Have students review the text if needed. A written assessment may be used to ensure understanding by all students, especially if not all participated.

Reflection

- Were the questions chosen by students thought provoking?
- How could you ensure participation of all students?
- What could you have done differently to make this activity more successful?
- What worked well?

Four-Corners Debate

LANGUAGE ARTS

SOCIAL STUDIES

SCIENCE

Four-Corners Debate is a strategy that allows discussion among students with differing opinions about an issue in a selected text. Students must support their ideas and opinions with evidence from the text. This strategy requires students to reflect on their reading, express their thoughts, listen to others, and draw conclusions.

Procedure

After reading a selected text, you make signs to place in each corner of the room. The signs read "Agree," "Disagree," "Strongly Agree," and "Strongly Disagree." You then place a statement on the board that requires students to have an opinion or reaction. Students move to the corner of the room that expresses their opinion to the statement and are given five minutes to discuss and choose a leader. Each group shares their opinions with the other groups. This is followed by time for student debate. Students may change corners at any time if they provide the reason why they decided to change.

Language Arts
Topic: *Anne Frank: The Diary of a Young Girl* **by Anne Frank**
Statement: Anne Frank had several options available to her that would have increased her ability to survive.

Social Studies
Topic: The Civil War
Statement: The United States would not have been as strong as it is today without the occurrence of the Civil War.

Science
Topic: Evolution
Statement: We can prove that we have evolved over time.

Assessment

Use your teacher observation throughout the statement of opinions to determine students' level of comprehension. Have students review the text if needed. Ensure students expressed their positions clearly, used appropriate logic, and addressed opposing viewpoints.

(continued)

Jonson, 2006

Reflection

- Did the chosen statement elicit varied opinions from the students?
- Were students able to adequately support their opinions and statements through information from the text?
- Were all students actively engaged?
- What could you have done differently to make this activity more successful?
- What worked well?

Group Investigation

This strategy allows each student to be personally responsible for a small portion of the information that is covered. Although students study and present their information only, they must listen and pay attention to the information presented by all other students. This is effective because students like to listen to their peers. This strategy is a powerful way to quickly cover a large amount of information.

Procedure

Students work in groups of two to six members. Discuss the main topic that is being covered in class. Each group then selects a subtopic related to the main topic, and each group member researches a portion of that topic. Students share their information within their group to ensure they have covered their individual topic well. Each group then presents its information to the entire class.

Language Arts
Main Topic: Parts of Speech
Subtopics: noun, pronoun, adjective, adverb, preposition

Social Studies
Main Topic: Earth's Physical Geography
Subtopics: land, air, water, climate, weather

Science
Main Topic: States of Matter
Subtopics: solids, liquids, gases

Assessment

Determine if complete and correct information was given in the class presentations. A written assessment also may be used.

Reflection

• Do you need to give more guidance to students regarding the subtopics chosen?

• How do you ensure that all students actively participate?

• How do you address information that was left out by group members to ensure all students have the necessary information to fully comprehend the text?

• What could you have done differently to make this activity more successful?

• What worked well?

Hendrix, 1999

LANGUAGE ARTS

SOCIAL STUDIES

SCIENCE

MATH

Jigsaw

Jigsaw allows students to work with their peers and to learn information from one another. This strategy allows for all members of the class to receive information about an entire section in a text. It is a collaborative strategy that ensures the participation of all students.

Procedure

First, place three to six students in teams. Give each team member a topic on which to become an "expert." The teams then split up and find the students from the other teams who are working on their topic. After working in the topic groups, students return to their teams and present the information they gained.

Language Arts
When reviewing a specific story, assign team members with a component such as character, plot, setting, problem, or resolution.

Social Studies
When studying the five themes of geography, assign each member of a team one of the topics: location, place, human-environment interaction, movement, or regions.

Science
Give each member of a group a topic such as acids, bases, or salts.

Math
Use as review. After studying fractions, divide into groups and assign each member a topic such as adding, subtracting, dividing, or multiplying.

Assessment

Determine students' level of comprehension by the correct number of responses in a quiz or through discussion of information presented by each team.

Reflection

• How could you ensure that all aspects of the topic are covered?

• How could you ensure that the quality of information remains constant among the groups?

• What could you have done differently to make this activity more successful?

• What worked well?

Aronson & Patnoe, 1997; Hendrix, 1999

Learning Together

LANGUAGE ARTS

SOCIAL STUDIES

SCIENCE

MATH

Students tend to feel more comfortable when they are able to work with others. This may lessen their anxiety and help them to learn more. The group sheet is a quick evaluation for student comprehension, but follow-up for individual accountability is necessary.

Procedure

Place students in small groups of four or five members. Have them work together on a worksheet that covers information that has either been instructed or is in the text. Everyone contributes and must know the information. At the end of the activity, the group submits a single worksheet.

Language Arts
Use this activity with parts of speech and grammar rules.

Social Studies/Science
Complete a worksheet or questions from the end of a chapter, or create your own worksheets to cover the information discussed.

Math
Complete worksheets that cover addition, subtraction, multiplication, or division of fractions.

Assessment

Determine students' comprehension by evaluating the group worksheet and giving individual quizzes.

Reflection

• How could you ensure that all group members comprehend the information fully?

• How could you ensure that all members participate equally?

• What could you have done differently to make this activity more successful?

• What worked well?

Hendrix, 1999

Partner Prediction

This strategy gives students the opportunity to work with their peers and make predictions about a story or section. Because students are sharing their ideas with a partner, more students are able to discuss prediction without being self-conscious about speaking in front of the entire class. If a student is having difficulties with prediction, partner him or her with someone who is able to do it, and he or she will have the opportunity to see how the process is done.

Procedure

First, identify places in the text to stop and predict what might happen next. Then read the title and first portion aloud and ask what students think the story is about. Students should be seated next to partners so they can share their ideas with each other. This process is repeated throughout the reading. When the end of the selection is near, stop and ask how students think it ends.

Language Arts
Topic: "Cats on the Run"
Students discuss what this story may be about. As reading begins, students learn it is about tigers in the wild. Students discuss what might happen in the story.

Social Studies
Topic: Japan
Students discuss what they know. Mention origami and ask students to discuss what they have learned to make or what they would like to learn. Reading covers haiku and the Japanese language.

Science
Topic: Plants
Students discuss what they know. Reading covers types of trees and flowers. Students discuss how to tell the difference among the types and which ones they have seen, and they discuss what else might be covered in the text.

Assessment

Through your teacher observation and discussion, determine accuracy of student predictions. Monitor the involvement of individual students during the paired retelling. Discussion can be used to determine students' level of comprehension by assessing their responses after reading. Encourage responses from students who appear off task. Students should correctly respond to questions during a discussion. Change partners to increase accuracy if necessary.

Buehl, 1997

Reflection

- Did you monitor well enough to know that all students were participating?
- Were students able to make reasonable predictions?
- What predictions did students make that were reasonable but unexpected?
- What could you have done differently to make this activity more successful?
- What worked well?

Peer-Assisted Learning Strategies (PALS)

PALS allow students to work with a partner. It focuses on teaching students a set of comprehension strategies that can be transferred to many different types of texts. (Although this strategy initially involves more teacher involvement and preparation than other strategies in this book, it is beneficial to include.) The majority of teacher involvement is in introducing the program with modeling, explanation, and guided practice. This strategy usually involves 30 minutes of class time three days a week. More information can be found at www.peerassistedlearningstrategies.net.

Procedure

Pair higher and lower readers with the roles of coach and reader. The text should be at the instructional level of the lower reader. Each student reads aloud for five minutes, starting with the higher reader. The lower reader then reads the same passage for five minutes. After five minutes, the lower reader retells the passage to the higher reader. The higher reader can prompt with questions as needed.

Next, the pair does paragraph shrinking to identify the main idea. Students shrink paragraphs by continuing the same passage but with no rereading. Each student reads one paragraph and tells the main idea. The higher reader again reads first.

Finally, the students participate in prediction relay. This is done with larger units of text and a new activity. In this activity, readers predict what happens next, accurately read half a page, accurately check the prediction, and correctly summarize the important information. This begins with the higher reader and continues for five minutes with each reader. Both correct word recognition errors as they occur.

Language Arts
This strategy is best used with short stories or long poems. Students can ask about vocabulary or concepts.

Social Studies/Science
Use with any selection of informational text. Assist students with vocabulary, concepts, or directions as needed.

Assessment

Use your teacher observation throughout the process to determine students' level of comprehension. Have students review the text if needed. Have coach readers submit guiding questions they used.

Fuchs, Fuchs, Mathes, & Simmons, 1997; Liang & Dole, 2006

Reflection

- Did you monitor enough to ensure both readers comprehended the text?
- Were all students able to make and check their predictions?
- How could you assist students who have difficulty reading half a page while correcting word recognition errors as they occurred?
- How could you ensure that students are able to summarize important information?
- How could you be certain students will be able to use this strategy successfully in the future?
- What could you have done differently to make this activity more successful?
- What worked well?

Reciprocal Teaching

This strategy allows students to begin to work together and to "teach" each other as they take over the discussion.

Procedure

Begin by dividing the class into small groups. Each group should then read and discuss a short section from the text. After all the groups are done, bring the entire class together and discuss the information that was covered. Start by leading the discussion, then gradually decrease your input and allow student input to increase. Encourage the participation of all students.

Language Arts
Topic: Short Section of a Story
Ask the following questions: Why did the main character react as he or she did? What is the importance of the setting in this story?

Social Studies
Topic: Earth's Human Geography
Ask the following questions: Where do people live? Why do they migrate? What problems will the growing population cause?

Science
Go over types of matter or ask, What is an ecosystem?

Assessment

Use discussion, quizzes, and observation to determine if material is understood. Observation should include monitoring the involvement of individual students and their responses. Discussion can be used to determine students' level of comprehension by assessing their responses after reading. Encourage responses from students who appear off task. Students should correctly respond to questions during a discussion or those given on a quiz. Encourage students to assist one another.

Reflection

- How can you guide students as they take on more of the teaching to make sure they are covering all material and asking higher order questions?
- What could you have done to increase student participation?
- What could you have done differently to make this activity more successful?
- What worked well?

Aarnoutse, Brand-Gruwel, & Oduber, 1997; Banikowski & Mehring, 1999; Palincsar, 1984

Save the Last Word for Me

LANGUAGE ARTS

SOCIAL STUDIES

SCIENCE

This strategy provides a structure for discussing information and ideas and making connections.

Procedure

Begin by assigning a passage to read. Have students choose five statements from the book to comment on. Comments can be anything, including things that surprised students, reminded them of something else, or were something they agreed or disagreed with.

Next, give each student five index cards, one for each comment. On the front, they write the actual statement from the text and on the back, they write their comment. Finally, the class is divided into groups. Students take turns in the group by reading a statement and allowing everyone to comment before they share their comment, or the last word. This continues so everyone has an opportunity to share statements and comments.

Language Arts
Statement: A summary combines important ideas of a chapter or idea into a paragraph.
Comment: Summaries can really help us when studying for a test.

Social Studies
Statement: More than three million people left their farms because of the Dust Bowl.
Comment: With so many people leaving, it would be hard to rebuild the farm areas.

Science
Statement: As water soaks through the soil, it can pick up chemicals, such as pesticides.
Comment: It is hard to know if our water is safe. People don't think about how they hurt others.

Assessment

Determine comprehension through questioning and observing discussions. Ensure that students show a deep understanding of the text.

Reflection

- How could you guide students to ensure that their comments lead to a deeper understanding of the text?
- What is the effect of listening on the students' comprehension?
- What could you have done differently to make this activity more successful?
- What worked well?

Buehl, 2009; McLaughlin & Allen, 2009; Short, Harste, & Burke, 1996; Vaughan & Estes, 1986

Silent With Support

This strategy involves allowing the students to read the text silently while sitting with partners or in small groups. As they read silently, the students should get help from those around them if needed. This strategy can be used in any subject area. It is important to group the students according to mixed ability.

Procedure

Place students in pairs or in small groups. Allow them to read the story or text selection silently while sitting with their partner or group. Explain that they may consult with their group if they have questions or need assistance during the reading.

Language Arts
Use the strategy with stories, poems, or grammar lessons. Students can ask about vocabulary, concepts, or directions.

Social Studies/Science
Use with any selection of text. Students may get assistance with vocabulary, concepts, or directions.

Math
Use with word problems.

Assessment

Determine comprehension through discussion, quizzes or tests, or your teacher questioning. Discussion and teacher questioning can be used to determine students' level of comprehension by assessing their responses after reading. Encourage responses from students who appear off task. Students should correctly respond to questions during a discussion or given on a quiz. If students are unable to respond correctly, you may want to regroup certain students to improve the support given by the partners.

Reflection

• How could you best group or pair students to ensure that they have enough support?
• What could you have done differently to make this activity more successful?
• What worked well?

Lamme & Beckett, 1992

Skit Performance

This strategy allows students to be involved in their learning. It provides cooperative learning because each student has a part to play in the story or contributes to the script writing. It is also useful for kinesthetic learners. Through their participation, students are able to demonstrate their understanding of the concepts covered.

Procedure

Students read a story or text, then write and perform a skit or play about the concepts they have studied. This does not need to be a major production (although you might want to occasionally allow students to make it into a public presentation or performance). It is just a way to determine if students understand what they read.

Language Arts	Social Studies
After studying a story, have students pretend to be characters from the story and give a general idea of the story or perform a scene.	After studying several cultures, have students pretend to be people from these cultures meeting for the first time, discussing similarities and differences.

Assessment

Determine comprehension through discussion and correct display of concepts. Discussion can be used to determine students' level of comprehension by assessing their responses after reading. Students should be able to communicate the main concepts in the text through their skit performance. If they are unable to do so, use discussion to reinforce the main concepts with the students and allow them to alter their skit to include the main concepts. This can also be assessed by having groups of students perform certain sections or stories for the entire class. Each group is given a list of concepts or questions that they need to cover during their performance to ensure understanding by the entire class. Quizzes or tests may also be used to assess understanding following the performance.

Reflection

- What role can be given to students who are not comfortable performing in front of students?
- Would this be beneficial as a filmed activity to review with the class?
- What could you have done differently to make this activity more successful?
- What worked well?

Cochran, 1993

LANGUAGE ARTS

SOCIAL STUDIES

SCIENCE

MATH

Student Teams—Achievement Division

This strategy is useful in reviewing information from a lesson and is most effective when the questions have a single correct answer. Students are able to work together cooperatively.

Procedure

After teaching a lesson, group students into four-member, mixed-ability teams. Each team works together to make certain that every member of the group has mastered the information. Use a quiz to go over the information and give an individual and team score.

The steps for this process are as follows:

1. Teach concept or skill—check understanding

2. Team study—rank students and group students as one high achiever, two average achievers, and one low achiever; teams complete worksheets and are responsible for all members mastering the concept

3. Test—check individual understanding; give team points based on improvement over previous average: 10 below average or more = 0 points; 10 below to 1 below average = 10 points; 0 to 10 above average = 20 points; more than 10 above average = 30 points

4. Team recognition for team with highest score

Giving team scores in addition to individual scores motivates the teams to make certain everyone understands the information that has been covered.

Language Arts
The strategy is best for information such as grammar or punctuation; students should go over the rules and correct usage.

Social Studies
Review and discuss the five themes of geography; students should be able to identify the five themes and characteristics of each.

Science
Using topics such as acids, bases, and salts, students should be able to identify properties of each and know how to determine where a substance belongs.

Math
The strategy works well with simple equations and problems; students may use flashcards or cover more difficult work using paper to solve the problems.

Hendrix, 1999; Nesbit & Rogers, 1997; Slavin, 1988

Assessment

Use discussion, quizzes, and tests to ascertain level of understanding. Discussion can be used to determine students' level of comprehension by assessing their responses after reading. Encourage responses from students who appear off task. Students should correctly respond to questions during a discussion or given on a quiz or test.

Reflection

- Would this strategy work well with larger groups?
- Would this strategy work well with pairs of students?
- What forms of reward could be used?
- How could you ensure that motivation remains high with all students?
- What could you have done differently to make this activity more successful?
- What worked well?

LANGUAGE ARTS

SOCIAL STUDIES

SCIENCE

MATH

Teams-Games-Tournament

Competition in the classroom can be motivational. Students work in teams, which promotes cooperative learning. Because of their competitive nature, students tend to cooperate with members of their team to prevail over the other teams.

Procedure

To use this strategy, place students homogeneously by past performance into groups of three or four. At the end of each week, hold a tournament based on the information that was covered during the week. Hold tournaments between teams of matched ability. Recognize the winning teams.

There is flexibility in organizing these tournaments. Change groups as necessary, but ensure that the groups are equally matched. A study period prior to the tournament allows students to go over the important information that was covered.

Language Arts
Topic: Vocabulary
Go over words or definitions, use synonyms, and fill in the blanks in sentences.

Social Studies
Topic: Immigrants to the United States
Discuss catastrophes in the 1880s, reasons immigrants came to the United States, and problems they encountered.

Science
Topic: States of Matter
Discuss solids, liquids, and gases and their properties.

Math
Topic: Geometry
Study shapes, area, volume, measurement, and formulas.

Assessment

Determine understanding through correct student responses in the tournament.

Reflection

• Were all students adequately involved?

• How might you change the teams to encourage participation?

• What could you have done differently to make this activity more successful?

• What worked well?

Hendrix, 1999

Think-Pair-Share/Think-Pair-Square

LANGUAGE ARTS

SOCIAL STUDIES

SCIENCE

MATH

This is a partner or group activity that allows students to work together to check for comprehension. This can be used with teacher-directed questions or with students as they read stories or sections of text.

Procedure

Pose a question to the class. Students think about the question individually, pair and discuss responses, and then share their responses or their partner's responses with other pairs (e.g., groups of four). Another way to use this strategy is after reading a story or text section. Students think of things they already know, decide what the reading reminds them of, and determine what might happen next. Students then "Pair and Share" (two students) or "Pair and Square" (four students) and discuss what they've thought about.

Language Arts
After covering a short story or selection, discuss character, plot, motivation, setting, and resolution.

Social Studies
After covering South America, discuss people, culture, religion, land, climate, and resources.

Science
After covering animal habitats, discuss what animals need to survive and how different animals adapt.

Math
After reading a word problem, determine what is being asked, what information is given, and what mathematical function or formula is needed to solve the problem.

Assessment

Use discussion, quizzes, or tests during or following the activity. Discussion can be used to determine students' level of comprehension by assessing their responses after reading. Encourage responses from students who appear off task. Students should correctly respond to questions during a discussion or given on a quiz or test.

Reflection

• What do you need to consider when pairing or grouping students?

• How might you expand this strategy to work with larger groups to incorporate the entire class (e.g., pairs, quads)?

• What could you have done differently to make this activity more successful?

• What worked well?

Banikowski & Mehring, 1999; Bromley & Modlo, 1997

Writing Word Problems

This strategy is useful in improving comprehension of word problems. Encouraging students to bring their cultures and background knowledge into the word problems helps them to become active participants in the learning process.

Procedure
Have students work in cooperative groups to create their own word problems that incorporate the concepts they have been studying. Assign roles in the groups if needed. Monitor the groups and let them know that each individual is accountable. As students are creating their problems, give feedback, making certain the problems are clear.

Math
After studying a section and dealing with word problems, have the students create word problems using their own age and circumstances with which they are familiar (movies, going out to eat, school).

Assessment

Have students from one group read their problem aloud while students from another group work out the problem on the chalkboard. This helps in determining if the problem is clear and contains all the necessary information. Evaluate the group that is presenting the problem as well as the group attempting to solve the problem.

Reflection

• What guidance did you need to give to ensure the creation of quality word problems?

• What could you have done differently to make this activity more successful?

• What worked well?

Muth, 1997; Winograd & Higgins, 1995

Connecting to Previous Knowledge

This section provides strategies that allow readers to connect the information they are reading to knowledge or interests they already have. If students are able to make connections, it is easier for them to see the relevance in much of the material that is covered. Often, students do not see the importance of a topic or do not have the necessary background information. In some cases, it may be helpful to provide some background knowledge that assists the students in comprehending the intended instructional material. Not all students come to the classroom with the same background knowledge, and any assistance we can provide is valuable. These strategies are especially useful in motivating students and creating interest in new topics.

Activate Prior Knowledge

LANGUAGE ARTS

SOCIAL STUDIES

SCIENCE

MATH

This strategy is designed to determine what students already know about the topic that is going to be studied. This helps to create interest prior to reading.

Activating prior knowledge allows students to feel that they are somehow connected to the topic being studied, helping to create a more positive learning environment and helping students feel that they are a part of the learning process.

Procedure

Before beginning a text, discuss the topic that is being covered. Have the students share what they already know about the topic. Find ways to relate the knowledge they have with the material that needs to be covered.

Language Arts
Topic: Story About Snakes
Ask students, What do you know about snakes? How can you tell if they are poisonous? What snakes are common in our area?

Social Studies
Topic: Climate
Ask students, How does climate affect vegetation? What kinds of plants grow in certain areas?

Science
Topic: Tornadoes
Ask students, What do you know about tornadoes? What do you know about thunderstorms? Are they similar? What would you do if you were caught in a tornado?

Math
Topic: Multiplication With Decimals
Ask students, When are decimals used in everyday life (e.g., money)? If you were purchasing several items at the same price, how could you quickly figure out the total cost?

Assessment

Discuss each question and determine from students' answers which students need additional information before beginning a lesson. As the lesson progresses, continue discussion and questions to determine students' comprehension of the topic.

Reflection

• What information should you have prepared before the lesson?

• How did providing students with prior knowledge assist them in comprehension?

• What could you have done differently to make this activity more successful?

• What worked well?

Bean & Zigmond, 1994; Pearson & Johnson, 1978; Vacca & Vacca, 1989

Analogy Charting

This strategy is designed to allow students to associate new learning with familiar concepts by perceiving similarities and differences in the concepts.

Procedure

You begin by choosing a familiar concept or story as a foundation for learning a new concept or story. Next, show the Analogy Chart and brainstorm similarities and differences with the class. Discuss how the similarities and differences relate to one another. Finally, have students independently write a summary statement about the new concept to demonstrate comprehension.

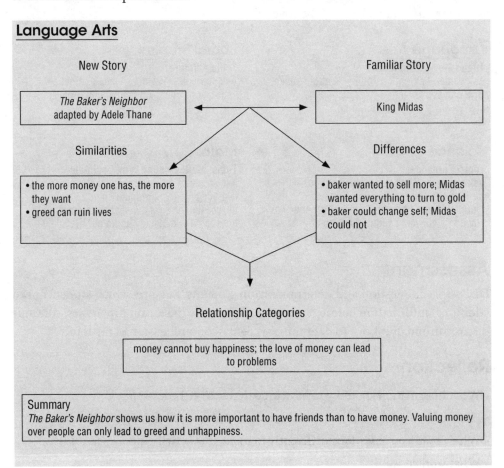

Language Arts

New Story

The Baker's Neighbor
adapted by Adele Thane

Familiar Story

King Midas

Similarities

• the more money one has, the more they want
• greed can ruin lives

Differences

• baker wanted to sell more; Midas wanted everything to turn to gold
• baker could change self; Midas could not

Relationship Categories

money cannot buy happiness; the love of money can lead to problems

Summary
The Baker's Neighbor shows us how it is more important to have friends than to have money. Valuing money over people can only lead to greed and unhappiness.

Buehl, 2009

Social Studies

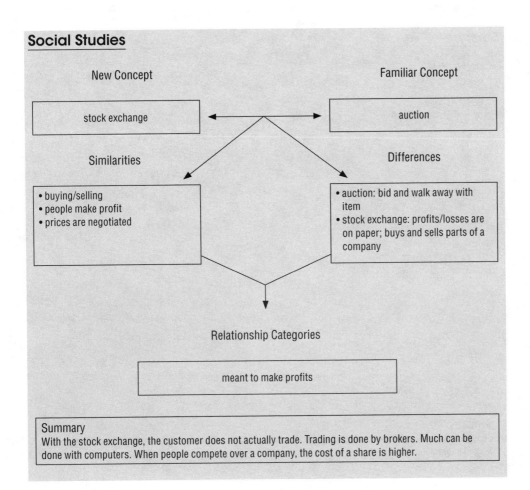

New Concept

stock exchange

Familiar Concept

auction

Similarities

- buying/selling
- people make profit
- prices are negotiated

Differences

- auction: bid and walk away with item
- stock exchange: profits/losses are on paper; buys and sells parts of a company

Relationship Categories

meant to make profits

Summary
With the stock exchange, the customer does not actually trade. Trading is done by brokers. Much can be done with computers. When people compete over a company, the cost of a share is higher.

(continued)

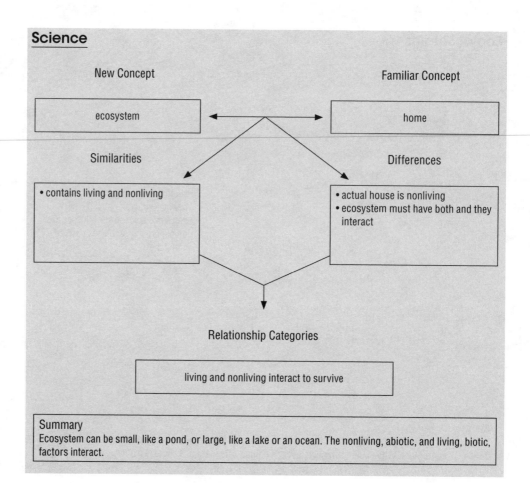

Science

New Concept

| ecosystem |

Familiar Concept

| home |

Similarities

- contains living and nonliving

Differences

- actual house is nonliving
- ecosystem must have both and they interact

Relationship Categories

| living and nonliving interact to survive |

Summary
Ecosystem can be small, like a pond, or large, like a lake or an ocean. The nonliving, abiotic, and living, biotic, factors interact.

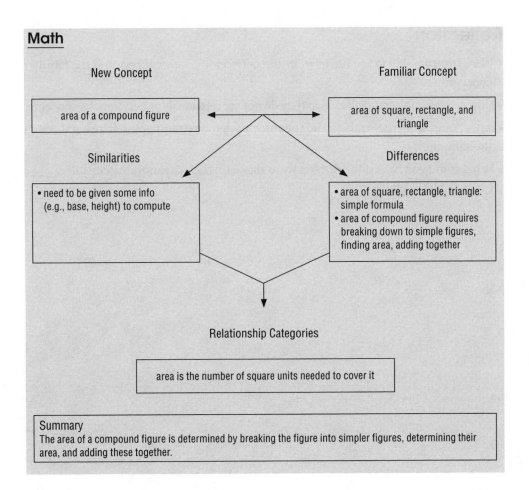

Math

New Concept

area of a compound figure

Familiar Concept

area of square, rectangle, and triangle

Similarities

- need to be given some info (e.g., base, height) to compute

Differences

- area of square, rectangle, triangle: simple formula
- area of compound figure requires breaking down to simple figures, finding area, adding together

Relationship Categories

area is the number of square units needed to cover it

Summary
The area of a compound figure is determined by breaking the figure into simpler figures, determining their area, and adding these together.

Assessment

Review student summaries to determine student comprehension. As necessary, continue discussions to enhance students' comprehension of the topic.

(continued)

Reflection

- Were students able to see the relationship between the new concept and the familiar concept?
- How can you assist students when they do not see relationships between the concepts?
- After completing the strategy, did the students demonstrate comprehension through the summary?
- What could you have done differently to make this activity more successful?
- What worked well?

Anticipation Guide

This strategy allows students to consider thoughts and opinions they have about various topics to create an interest in the material that is being covered and to establish a purpose for reading the material.

This strategy works best with topics such as literature, science, and social studies that require information to develop opinions. Although subjects such as grammar and mathematics are more skill related, there are instances in which a modified Anticipation Guide would be useful.

Procedure

Begin by listing three or more debatable statements about a topic that students are going to study. Ask the students to identify whether they agree or disagree with the statements. Explain that the students need to read the text carefully and see if they can find statements that support their own views. After they read the text, discuss the original statements to see if the students maintain their original view or if they have changed their opinion.

When constructing an Anticipation Guide, keep the following in mind:

- Analyze the material and determine main ideas.
- Write the ideas in short, declarative statements. Avoid abstractions.
- Put the statements in a format that encourages anticipation and predictions.
- Discuss readers' predictions and anticipations before reading.
- Assign the text. Have students evaluate the statements according to the author's intent and purpose.
- Contrast the predictions with the author's intended meaning.

Language Arts

Topic:	**Writing a persuasive paper**
Statements:	Students should wear uniforms in school.
	Students should be allowed to choose whatever classes they want to take.
	There should be no dress code in schools.

Social Studies

Topic:	**Ancient Mediterranean civilization**
Statements:	Living in the ancient Mediterranean civilization was rewarding for all people.
	Ancient writing is similar to our writing of today.
	There were no schools in ancient civilizations.

(continued)

Banikowski & Mehring, 1999; Gunning, 1996; Herber, 1978; Vacca & Vacca, 1989

Topic: **Plant life**
Statements: All types of plants can be grown anywhere.
              Poisonous plants are easy to identify.
              All plants come from seeds.

Assessment

After discussing each statement, listening to student responses, and reading the text, review the statements again to see if students are able to support their response to the statements.

Reflection

• How could you ensure that the statements given to students help to improve their comprehension?

• Could you use this as a foundation to teach the concept of debate?

• What could you have done differently to make this activity more successful?

• What worked well?

Brainstorming

LANGUAGE ARTS

SOCIAL STUDIES

SCIENCE

This strategy allows students to share their knowledge and experiences related to a topic by creating interest in the text. The strategy facilitates comprehension by activating prior knowledge; however, it is more structured than the Activate Prior Knowledge strategy.

Brainstorming is most effective when a topic is given and students state things that they think are related to the topic. A limited amount of time should be given for this activity before continuing with a discussion.

Procedure

Begin by listing words or concepts that are in the text. Then ask students to identify what they already know about these—in writing or orally. This can be done individually, in small groups, or in a large group. Share all the information with the entire class before reading the text. Add information to help students better understand the concepts.

Language Arts
Before reading a story about fantastic creatures, brainstorm the following:
- what is fantasy
- creatures
- fantasy creatures (e.g., the Loch Ness Monster)

Social Studies
Before reading about Egypt, brainstorm the following:
- pyramids
- mummies
- workers
- pharaohs

Science
Before reading about types of solutions, brainstorm the following:
- colloids and suspensions
- concentrates
- saturation

Assessment

After reading the text, review the words or concepts that were covered originally. Then ask students to identify new information they learned that was not listed in the Brainstorming activity.

(continued)

Banikowski & Mehring, 1999; Cochran, 1993; Vacca & Vacca, 1989

Reflection

- How effective would it be to let students brainstorm in pairs or small groups and then share with the whole class?
- How might you ensure input from each student in this activity?
- What could you have done differently to make this activity more successful?
- What worked well?

Directed Reading Activity (DRA)

Often students are instructed to read without being told why the information is important or what they are expected to learn. DRA provides students with a purpose for reading using the sharing of previous knowledge to build understanding.

Procedure

The components of this activity are as follows:

- Before reading (Prereading)—Establish purpose, build background, and motivate.
- During reading (Reader–Text Interactions)—Prompt active response for reading.
- After reading (Postreading)—Reinforce and extend ideas.

First, go over key concepts and vocabulary words. Next, tell students why the information is needed (e.g., for a test, quiz, grade, demonstration) and what information you would like them to acquire. Then allow the students to read silently.

Finally, have a follow-up activity such as a demonstration, speech, questions, or quiz. The follow-up activity can be extended by linking it to other activities or assignments.

Language Arts
- Tell students they will explore different types of poems before they are asked to write a poem of their own.
- Go over related vocabulary.
- Have students read the selection independently.
- Have students volunteer to read aloud with expression.
- Give assignment to write poem.

Social Studies
- Pose this question to students: If history repeats itself, will what happened to the Roman Empire possibly happen to the United States?
- Go over vocabulary.
- Give a test or quiz.
- Give students sections of text and have them make posters to discuss.
- Link to politics.

Science
- Have students think of impressive views of landscapes they have seen, and explain that you will cover various types of landscapes.
- Go over vocabulary such as *landforms, constellations, contour lines, elevation, latitude, longitude.*
- Link to geography and social studies.

Math
- Tell students the information they will be learning will be used throughout their lives, especially when purchasing items and balancing a checkbook.
- Go over integers and the concept of negative and positive.
- Explain that they will be working in pairs to try to balance an imaginary checkbook.

(continued)

Cochran, 1993; Gunning, 1996; Vacca & Vacca, 1989

Assessment

Through the follow-up activity, questions, and discussion, determine students' comprehension of the given topic. The follow-up activity and discussion can be used to determine students' level of comprehension by assessing their responses. Encourage responses from students who appear off task. Students should correctly respond to questions during a discussion or given on a quiz or test. If students do not respond correctly, provide additional instruction and information. Students may be allowed to work together if necessary.

Reflection

- Were your students able to gain adequate comprehension from this strategy?
- What information should you have prepared to assist students?
- How could you help students to extend the ideas?
- What could you have done differently to make this activity more successful?
- What worked well?

FLIP

LANGUAGE ARTS

SOCIAL STUDIES

SCIENCE

MATH

This strategy is used before reading to determine the friendliness, language, interest, and prior knowledge regarding a reading selection. Once the students have discussed their prior knowledge about the selection, they may feel more interested in the topic and be able to contribute to a discussion.

Procedure

The steps for this strategy are as follows:

- [F]riendliness—Determine what features are easy to understand (friendly) and difficult to understand (unfriendly).
- [L]anguage—Determine what terms the students might need to learn more about.
- [I]nterest—Determine the level of interest, which may affect the level of involvement.
- [P]rior Knowledge—Determine what the students already know about what is being asked.

Discuss each of these areas with the students and determine ways to improve the areas that might cause difficulty. For example, if the features make reading difficult, discuss headings, paragraphs, and layout to decide how to make it friendlier. Occasionally, it will be evident that some of the terms need to be discussed prior to reading. If the level of interest is not high, find ways to relate some part of the selection to the students to give them more motivation to read. You may choose to have students create a graphic organizer on their papers with headings for each section in order to ensure participation.

Language Arts
Topic: *Maniac Magee* by Jerry Spinelli
F—The story has a fairly easy reading level.
L—Locate words such as *maniac*.
I—Discuss what it would be like to grow up on your own.
P—Ask students if they know children like Maniac Magee.

Social Studies
Topic: Early African Civilizations
F—The text is divided into sections.
L—Introduce words such as *civilization*.
I—Discuss how early civilizations affect present-day society.
P—Discuss what students already know about African civilizations.

(continued)

Fuentes, 1998

Science

Topic: Nature of Light

F—The text is divided into sections with questions.

L—Go over words such as *opaque, translucent,* and *transparent.*

I—Think how fast light moves.

P—Ask what students already know about light.

Math

Topic: Decimals

F—Words are easy to understand.

L—Students need to recognize decimals and what they mean.

I—Show interest when related to money.

P—Discuss use of decimals in money.

Assessment

After the FLIP strategy, determine if additional language needs to be introduced and if more interest should be developed. Discussion and questions can be used to determine students' level of comprehension by assessing their responses after reading. You should encourage responses from students who appear off task. Students should correctly respond to questions in a discussion or on a quiz or test. Review specific steps in FLIP for students who do not give correct answers.

Reflection

• Were your students able to gain adequate comprehension from this strategy?

• How much of this strategy should be teacher-directed?

• What could you have done differently to make this activity more successful?

• What worked well?

Gallery Images

This strategy allows students to create mental images while reading to assist in comprehension.

It works best with informational topics such as literature, science, and social studies. Although subjects such as grammar and mathematics are more skill related, there are instances in which a modified Gallery Images would be useful.

Procedure

Begin by explaining the concept of using visual images to represent information. Show examples. Have students work in small groups as they read selected text. Tell them to create mental images as they read. Have groups create posters with two to four images and ask students to label their text. Next, have groups share their images and labels with the class. Finally, have students work as individuals or in groups to create images in various content areas.

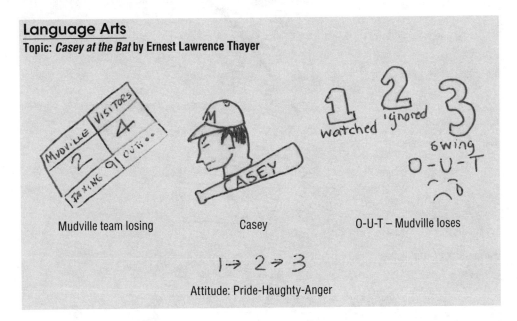

Language Arts
Topic: *Casey at the Bat* by Ernest Lawrence Thayer

Mudville team losing   Casey   O-U-T – Mudville loses

Attitude: Pride-Haughty-Anger

McLaughlin & Allen, 2009; Ogle, 2000

(continued)

Social Studies
Topic: Egyptian Society
Pharaoh

Nobles (officials, priests)

Scribes/Craftspeople

Farmers/Servants/Slaves

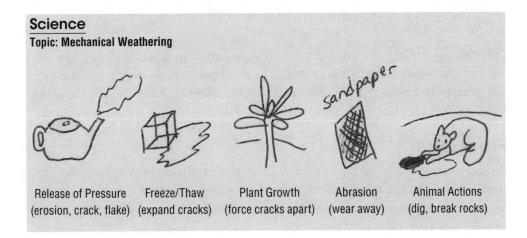

Science
Topic: Mechanical Weathering

| Release of Pressure (erosion, crack, flake) | Freeze/Thaw (expand cracks) | Plant Growth (force cracks apart) | Abrasion (wear away) | Animal Actions (dig, break rocks) |

Assessment

After reviewing gallery images and listening to student descriptions, determine if students are able to make connections and show comprehension of the selection.

Reflection

• How can you assist students who have difficulty finding images to represent concepts?

• What could you have done differently to make this activity more successful?

• What worked well?

Interactive Notation System to Effective Reading and Thinking

This strategy provides students with opportunities for reflection and allows them to connect prior knowledge to text content. The strategy facilitates comprehension by activating prior knowledge; however, it also allows students to determine parts of the text that contradict what they thought they knew, is new to them, or confuses them.

Procedure

Begin by introducing the topic to be studied. Have students brainstorm what they already know about the topic. Next, teach the notation system: ✓ (check mark) confirms what you know; − (minus sign) contradicts what you know; + (plus sign) is new to you; ? (question mark) confuses you.

Students use the notation system with the text by writing on a selection, in the margins, or using sticky notes. This can be done with a text you have selected and can be done by individual students. This helps them to determine what additional information is needed, what questions need to be answered, or what new questions may result. Once understood, students may use this strategy independently to assist in comprehending texts in other assignments.

Social Studies
Cuba lies about 90 miles south of Florida. ✓
It is one of the world's top producers of sugar, and most of the farms are owned and operated by the government. +

Science
Weathering occurs when rocks and other substances break down at the earth's surface. ✓
Erosion occurs when wind, water, ice, or gravity move rock particles. +
If a rock is broken into smaller pieces, it is mechanical weathering. ?

Math
When line segments or rays intersect and form angles ✓ that are 90°, the lines are perpendicular. ✓
Parallel lines never intersect but are in the same plane. +
Skew lines never intersect, are not parallel, and lie in different planes. + ?

Buehl, 2009; Vaughan & Estes, 1986

Assessment

After reading the text, review the words or concepts that were new to students or that confused them. Then ask students to identify new questions that came out of the activity. The type of questions they identify indicates their level of comprehension.

Reflection

- How effective was the strategy with your students?
- Did you provide enough information regarding the notations to ensure that your students were not hindered trying to recall them or making sure they used all of them?
- What should you do if students do not find any parts of the text that confirm what they already know?
- What could you have done differently to make this activity more successful?
- What worked well?

List-Group-Label

List-Group-Label provides students with a framework to connect to prior knowledge and show relationships within topics.

Procedure

Begin by explaining and modeling List-Group-Label. This is a simple brainstorming strategy that stresses relationships between words. Once students understand the strategy, write a word or phrase on the board. Have students brainstorm words or concepts related to the topic. Discuss if any should be eliminated and why. As a class or small group, have students group or cluster words and give a heading. Students should be able to explain reasons they chose the groupings. Read the text, then revisit the clusters and modify.

Social Studies

Dust Bowl

Location	Cause	Effect
Great Plains	drought	top soil dries out and blows away
		people move away

Science

Waste Disposal and Recycling

Ways to handle waste	Items to recycle	How people can control waste
burn	metal	reduce
bury (landfill)	plastic	reuse
recycle	glass	recycle
	paper	

Assessment

After reading the text, have students share their List-Group-Label and discuss. Ask questions related to the text. If students do not respond correctly, provide additional instruction and information. Students may be allowed to work together if necessary.

Buehl, 2009; Maring, Furman, & Blum-Anderson, 1985

Reflection

- How could you promote ways for students to come up with enough words or phrases to group?
- Were students able to independently see relationships in order to group words, or did they require a great deal of guidance?
- How could you assist students in using this strategy on their own in the future?
- What could you have done differently to make this activity more successful?
- What worked well?

Nonfiction Trade Books

After introducing a selected topic, use nonfiction trade books to help students expand their knowledge on that particular topic. Reading material that is appropriate for their individual reading levels helps students to be successful readers by decreasing the frustration that might exist with material that is too advanced. Also, relating this reading material to information that was previously covered enables students to make a connection with this knowledge.

Procedure

Begin by locating trade books that relate to the class topic, and make these available to the students. These books may help students to relate to the topic and learn information that they might be able to share with the class. It is important to be aware of the reading level of each trade book; do not choose levels that would be too challenging for the student because this will only discourage them.

Social Studies
Read trade books about different cultures, languages, and religions.

Science
Read books about earthquakes, volcanoes, moving water, plants, and animals.

Assessment

Through discussion, quizzes, and individual reports, assess students' knowledge regarding the topic. Discussion can be used to determine students' level of comprehension by assessing their responses after reading. Encourage responses from students who appear off task. Students should correctly respond to questions during a discussion or given on a quiz. Individual reports can also assist the teacher in assessing students' level of comprehension.

Reflection

- Did you have enough books on varied levels?
- What new books could you introduce the next time?
- What are some other activities you could do for assessment?
- What could you have done differently to make this activity more successful?
- What worked well?

Manning, 1999a

Prediction Log

This strategy acts as a motivator and gives purpose to the reading. It also allows the students to be honest in their prediction and to do a self-evaluation. Based on what students have learned in previous years, they are able to make predictions.

Procedure

The first step in this strategy is to ask a question related to the topic of study, such as What was daily life like in Ancient Egypt? Next, have students write their predictions in a log. After reading the text, have students write in their logs what the answer is and if they were correct in their prediction. Collect the logs periodically to see if there are students who are having difficulties with this skill.

Language Arts
After reading about people from different backgrounds, ask, What would it be like to visit someone nearby who lives in a totally different way than you? What might he or she be like?

Social Studies
What was daily life like in Ancient Egypt?
What particles can be carried by wind?
How do sand dunes move?
What types of damage can be caused by the wind?

Assessment

Comprehension is determined through your evaluation of a logical prediction. This must be done on an individual basis using students' logs.

Reflection

• As students review their predictions and determine accuracy, how could you use this as an opportunity to show the benefit of self-evaluation by students?

• How accurate were students' predictions?

• What could you have done differently to make this activity more successful?

• What worked well?

Ivey, 1999a; Vacca & Vacca, 1989

LANGUAGE ARTS

SOCIAL STUDIES

SCIENCE

ReQuest

This strategy encourages students to build on previous knowledge and think about what might be important information in the assigned reading. It also gives them the opportunity to write questions about things they do not understand. One of the advantages to this strategy is that it breaks the text into short sections so it is not overwhelming to students.

Procedure

The first step is to choose the text to be covered. Make sure the text builds on previous knowledge. Next, have the students read the first paragraph or short section and have them think of questions to ask about the topic as they read. After the reading, have students ask their questions and use the text to answer. Next, ask higher level questions you have prepared. Continue reading the entire selection and have a question–answer session at the end of each section.

Language Arts

Read the introduction to a story. Have students ask questions about the characters, setting, and plot. Continue reading short sections. Prepare questions such as Do you think the characters are acting in the way they should? Why or why not? What would you have done in this situation? What is one thing that could have changed the entire outcome of this story?

Social Studies

Read the beginning of a chapter on the Fertile Crescent. Ask why it was called this. What is known about this area from long ago? End with questions such as What do you think caused this culture to last throughout time?

Science

When discussing a topic such as sound waves, ask students how they think Helen Keller learned to speak or how Ludwig van Beethoven was able to compose music even after he became deaf.

Assessment

Discuss and evaluate your and your students' questions and answers. Discussion can be used to determine students' level of comprehension by assessing their responses after reading. Encourage responses from students who appear off task. Students should correctly respond to questions during a discussion.

Gunning, 1996; Manzo, 1969; Vacca & Vacca, 1989

Reflection

• Were your students able to gain adequate comprehension from this strategy?

• How could you use this as a class activity?

• How might you chunk this into manageable sections?

• As students become more competent, might you increase the amount of each section?

• What could you have done differently to make this activity more successful?

• What worked well?

Story Content Instruction

This strategy uses students' existing knowledge as a framework for introducing the story, helping students relate more to the story and feel that they can contribute to the discussion.

Procedure

Prior to reading, give intensive instruction about potentially difficult parts of the story or text, including vocabulary or terminology. Relate each part to things the students already know. After completing this, have students read the story or text and discuss.

Language Arts
Topic: Family
Discuss what students consider to be a family. Have them describe their families.

Social Studies
Topic: Hindu religion in India
Discuss the importance of religion and various religions; describe religions students are familiar with in their community.

Science
Topic: Metamorphosis
Discuss the various cartoons and videos dealing with characters that "morph" (e.g., Animorphs).

Assessment

Through discussion, determine what knowledge students have regarding the topic.

Reflection

- Would it be effective to have the information shared in small groups with a group leader if the information were provided to them?
- What preparation was most helpful in understanding of the selection?
- What could you have done differently to make this activity more successful?
- What worked well?

Dole, Brown, & Woodrow, 1996

Story Impressions

This strategy is used with narrative selections. It provides a framework for narrative writing and encourages predictions about the story. Depending on the chosen words or phrases, students may also make connections between vocabulary and structure by referring to prior knowledge and general story structures (e.g., setting, character, problem, events, solution).

Procedure

Choose 5–10 words or phrases that provide clues about the story. These should relate to narrative elements such as characters, setting, problems, attempts to resolve, and resolution. List the words or phrases in the order they appear in the story. Have students use the word list of clues to write a Story Impression that tells what they think happens in the story. Have students share. Finally, read the original story and have students compare and contrast their Story Impressions with the original text.

Language Arts

The Baker's Neighbor adapted by Adele Thane
Town, bakery, pastries, rich baker scowling, thief for smelling, judge to decide, judge gave money to baker, took away, gave lesson

Assessment

After reading the original text and comparing and contrasting it with the Story Impressions, determine student comprehension regarding the text through questioning and discussion.

Reflection

- How close to the actual story were the students' impressions?
- How might students use this strategy themselves after reading a story to show comprehension?
- What could you have done differently to make this activity more successful?
- What worked well?

Buehl, 2009; McGinley & Denner, 1987

Improving Organization

This section provides strategies for helping students to organize material in a way that improves their comprehension. Many students become discouraged or confused when they have an abundance of information to learn and do not know how to put it in a format that helps with comprehension. These strategies incorporate the use of outlines, charts, and graphic organizers. Although many of the strategies require initial instruction in order for students to understand the steps involved, the strategies included here are ones that students can transfer to a variety of situations and they can choose those that are most beneficial to them. Our goal is to provide them with the necessary tools to not only to be successful in the classroom at the moment but also to be successful lifelong learners.

B/D/A Questioning Charts

This strategy prompts students to ask questions before, during, and after reading. It provides a visual organizer that helps to clarify and organize certain elements throughout the reading process.

Procedure

Begin by modeling the process for students. The basic steps involved are as follows:

1. Ask questions to clarify or deepen understanding about the selection that is going to be read. These should be both thick and thin questions. (See the Thick and Thin Questions strategy in Section Five.) Thin questions clarify what the author is writing about and thick questions ponder deeper questions. These are recorded in the "Before Reading" column.

2. Read short sections and add questions that come up to the "During Reading" column.

3. After reading the entire selection, write out lingering questions that can be discussed in the "After Reading" column. After all discussions have been completed, summarize what is now understood that was unclear before.

Language Arts
Topic: Diamante

B/D/A Questioning Chart What were you wondering?		
Before Reading	During Reading	After Reading
• What is a diamante? • How do diamantes compare with other type poems?	• What has to be in each line?	• Can you make a diamante with words that are not opposites?
What do you understand now that you didn't understand before? A diamante is a diamond-shaped poem that has seven lines. Lines 1 and 7 are opposite nouns. Lines 2–6 describe the nouns and have special rules for each line.		

(continued)

Buehl, 2009; Laverick, 2002

Social Studies
Topic: Electoral college

B/D/A Questioning Chart What were you wondering?		
Before Reading	During Reading	After Reading
• What is an electoral college? • How would our political system be different if we did not have an electoral college?	• Why do different states have a different number of votes?	• Why don't they just use the popular vote?
What do you understand now that you didn't understand before? The electoral college allows smaller states in rural areas to have a say in government. The number of electors is based on the population in each state.		

Science
Topic: Sound characteristics

B/D/A Questioning Chart What were you wondering?		
Before Reading	During Reading	After Reading
• What is pitch? • What aspects of pitch in our environment can we control?	• What makes a pitch high or low?	• How are pitches changed?
What do you understand now that you didn't understand before? Pitch can be high or low and can be changed by changing the length of something (e.g., guitar string, rubber band).		

Math

Topic: Metric capacity

B/D/A Questioning Chart What were you wondering?		
Before Reading	During Reading	After Reading
• What is meant by metric capacity? • Why do we not use the metric measuring system in all things in the United States?	• What are equivalent amounts?	• What are the metric units used for capacity?
What do you understand now that you didn't understand before? Metric capacity is measured with milliliter (drop), liter (soda bottle), and kiloliter (small pool).		

Assessment

Through comparison of the questions and the "What do you understand now that you didn't understand before?" section, discussion, and a quiz or test, determine if students have learned the information they originally wanted to know about. If there are still items they want to learn additional information about, discuss this with them or provide additional information.

Reflection

• What level of questioning was used by students?

• How could you encourage students to increase their depth of understanding of a text with this strategy?

• What could you have done differently to make this activity more successful?

• What worked well?

Character Perspective Charting

This strategy gives students a visual organizer that shows the relationship between a character's perspective and the events in a story. Adding characters' perspectives can clarify why they reacted in certain ways in the story, which gives more depth to the characters.

Procedure

After the students have read the entire story, they should use a map or chart to list the important events (e.g., problems, resolution). Assign each student to one character. Students discuss the characters' perspectives during each of the events in the story on the map or chart. Ask questions to focus on the characters' motives and reactions.

Language Arts
Character: _____

Perspective
Thoughts/feelings: _____
_____

Motivation: _____
_____
_____

Events
Problem: _____
_____

Resolution: _____
_____

Outcome: _____
_____

Social Studies
Character: Abraham Lincoln

Perspective
Thoughts/feelings: _____
_____

Motivation: _____
_____
_____

Events
Problem: _____
_____

Resolution: _____
_____

Outcome: _____
_____

Assessment

Through discussion and evaluation of the completed maps or charts, determine if students correctly identify the motives and reactions of characters. Discuss how the perception of a character relates to their motivation and actions.

Emery, 1996; Shanahan & Shanahan, 1997

Reflection

- Are there ways to enhance this strategy (e.g., letting some students perform) to make it more effective?
- What could you have done differently to make this activity more successful?
- What worked well?

Concept/Definition Mapping

This is a visual strategy used to enrich the understanding of a concept or definition. This can be done as an individual or group activity.

Procedure

Begin by showing a blank Concept/Definition map and review the three questions: What is it? What is it like? What are some examples? Present a new term or concept from the text and have students work in pairs or groups to fill out the information on the map. Instruct them to use the text, background knowledge, or other sources while completing the map.

After the three questions have been answered, have students write their definition in the explanation box. Explain that the definition should include several sentences and information from the map rather than be a definition as from a dictionary. Share the definitions and discuss.

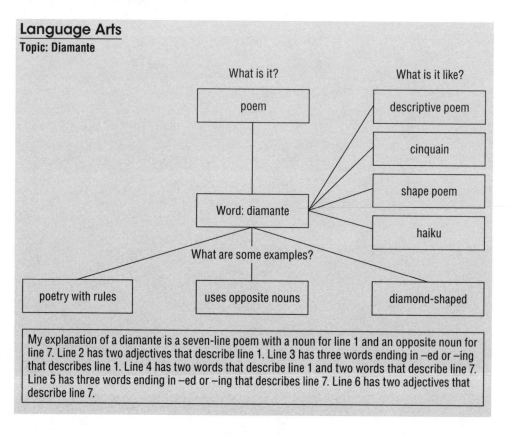

Language Arts
Topic: Diamante

What is it?

What is it like?

poem

descriptive poem

cinquain

shape poem

Word: diamante

haiku

What are some examples?

poetry with rules

uses opposite nouns

diamond-shaped

My explanation of a diamante is a seven-line poem with a noun for line 1 and an opposite noun for line 7. Line 2 has two adjectives that describe line 1. Line 3 has three words ending in –ed or –ing that describes line 1. Line 4 has two words that describe line 1 and two words that describe line 7. Line 5 has three words ending in –ed or –ing that describes line 7. Line 6 has two adjectives that describe line 7.

Buehl, 1995; Buehl, 2009; Schwartz & Raphael, 1985

Social Studies

Topic: Dictator

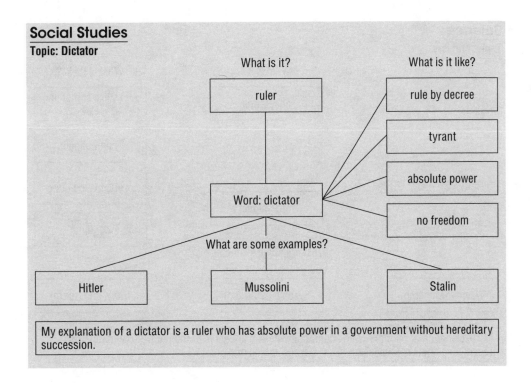

What is it?

ruler

What is it like?

rule by decree

tyrant

absolute power

no freedom

Word: dictator

What are some examples?

Hitler

Mussolini

Stalin

My explanation of a dictator is a ruler who has absolute power in a government without hereditary succession.

(continued)

Science
Topic: Mimicry

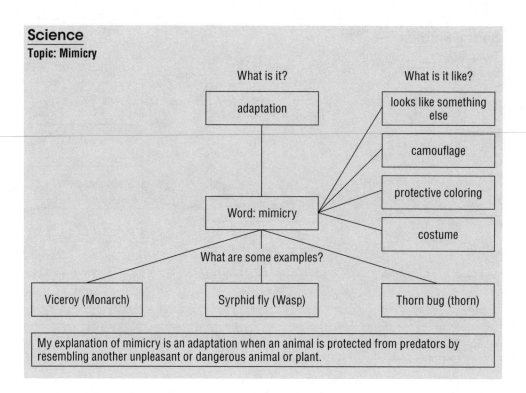

What is it?

adaptation

What is it like?

looks like something else

camouflage

protective coloring

costume

Word: mimicry

What are some examples?

Viceroy (Monarch)

Syrphid fly (Wasp)

Thorn bug (thorn)

My explanation of mimicry is an adaptation when an animal is protected from predators by resembling another unpleasant or dangerous animal or plant.

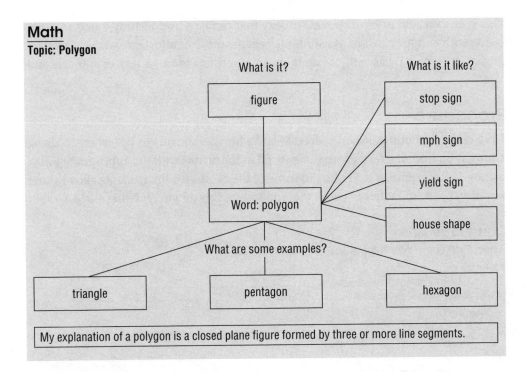

Math
Topic: Polygon

What is it?

figure

What is it like?

stop sign

mph sign

yield sign

house shape

Word: polygon

What are some examples?

triangle

pentagon

hexagon

My explanation of a polygon is a closed plane figure formed by three or more line segments.

Assessment

Assess students' explanations of their organizers and evaluate the information included in the organizer to determine comprehension.

Reflection

- Were students able to answer all of the questions?
- How much assistance was required for students to fill out the map?
- Did students demonstrate understanding of the text?
- What could you have done differently to make this activity more successful?
- What worked well?

Expectation Outline

This is an excellent organizational strategy that can be a useful study guide and that assists with comprehension. As students become more comfortable with the outline format, they may be able to create their own outlines for a variety of subjects and topics.

Procedure

First, create an outline, leaving several blanks for the students to use when covering information from the text. Have students fill in the blanks with the appropriate information as they come to it. (Filling in some of the blanks for the students allows those who may have difficulties to check their understanding of what is being asked.)

Language Arts
Topic: Short Story "Your Three Minutes Are Up"

I. Recall
    A. Libby wanted _____
    B. Her parents decided to _____

II. Interpreting
    A. Her parents _____ fair because _____
    B. Libby's friends were mad because _____

III. Evaluating
    A. Other alternatives that might have been used _____
    B. Lesson from the story _____

Social Studies
Topic: East Asia's Physical Geography

I. Land and water
    A. Physical features
    B. _____

II. Climate and _____
    A. Weather _____ - _____
    B. Storms _____ - _____

III. _____
    A. Minerals _____
    B. Forests _____

Vacca & Vacca, 1989

Science

Topic: States of Matter

I. Solid - _____
    A. Characteristics
        1. _____
        2. _____
    B. Examples
        1. ice
        2. _____

II. _____ - _____
    A. Characteristics
        1. _____
        2. _____
    B. Examples
        1. water
        2. _____

III. _____ - _____
    A. Characteristics
        1. _____
        2. _____
    B. Examples
        1. steam
        2. _____

Assessment

Determine if students have correctly covered the information by evaluating the completed outline and discussing the information. Discussion can be used to determine students' level of comprehension by assessing their responses after reading. Students should correctly respond to questions during a discussion or those given in their outline.

Reflection

- Would it be possible to have students create the initial outline for this strategy?
- What could you have done differently to make this activity more successful?
- What worked well?

Inquiry Charts

Inquiry Charts, also known as I-Charts, allow students to obtain knowledge based on curiosity rather than collecting random bits of knowledge. The chart prompts meaningful questions to guide research and organize writing. They can be used with the whole class, small groups, or individuals.

Procedure

Select a topic and list things that students may be curious about. Model how to use the chart. Brainstorm what is already known about the topic. Have access to various materials and sources of information, then fill out the chart as research is done. Summarize the information.

Language Arts

Topic: Persuasive Writing	Q1 What do we need to know?	Q2 How do we persuade others?	Q3 What are types of persuading?	Other Important Information	New Questions
What we know	Who we are writing to	Convince them	Speech, review, commercial, editorial	How can we convince others?	What is the difference in the types of writings?
Source textbook	Know who you are persuading				
Source writing handbook	Understand both sides of an argument in order to better support your side				
Source website	Preparation is key				
Summary	Get as much knowledge as possible about your audience, your topic, and opposing views before beginning				

Buehl, 2009; Hoffman, 1992

Social Studies

Topic: Urbanization	Q1 What is urbanization?	Q2 Why did people begin urbanization?	Q3 What were problems with it?	Other Important Information	New Questions
What we know	Movement of people from rural to cities	Fewer farmers needed because of machines	Fast growth; crowded conditions	Industrialization created jobs in cities	What troubles did people face in cities as populations grew?
Source textbook		Changes in technology impact changes in living situations			
Source reference book		People moved to cities for more conveniences			
Source website		Machines replaced workers in rural areas			
Summary		Because of advances in machinery, large numbers of people were replaced with machines. This caused people to move from rural areas to cities.			

(continued)

Science

Topic: Earth's crust	Q1 What makes the crust move?	Q2 What forces act on the crust?	Q3 What shapes the earth's surface?	Other Important Information	New Questions
What we know	Faults	Tension, compression	Water, wind, weather	There are many factors that cause mountains to form	How similar is the surface of the earth and moon?
Source textbook			Nature can affect the surface of the earth		
Source reference book			Water, wind, and the weather can cause erosion		
Source website			Erosion is one way the shape of the earth can change		
Summary			There are a variety of natural forces, including wind, water, and weather, that can change the shape of the earth.		

Math

Topic: Graphing	Q1 What is a line graph?	Q2 What is a bar graph?	Q3 What is a circle graph?	Other Important Information	New Questions
What we know	Shows how data changes over time	Allows comparison of facts about groups of data	Shows how parts relate to whole	In various types of graphs, the key is important.	How can you determine which graph is best to create?
Source textbook				The key shows the values of symbols	
Source reference book				Keys are necessary in order to interpret graphs accurately	
Source website				There are a variety of ways to create keys for graphs	
Summary				When creating a graph, it is important to use a key that enables the reader to accurately interpret information in the graph.	

Assessment

Assess students' explanations of their organizers and evaluate the information included in the organizer to determine comprehension.

(continued)

Reflection

- Were the questions chosen varied enough to encourage both recall and higher order thinking?
- How would you handle student who did not know anything about a given topic?
- What could you have done differently to make this activity more successful?
- What worked well?

Know-Want to Know-Learned (K-W-L)

LANGUAGE ARTS

SOCIAL STUDIES

SCIENCE

MATH

K-W-L gives students a purpose for reading and gives them an active role before, during, and after reading. This strategy helps them to think about the information they already know and to celebrate the learning of new information. It also strengthens their ability to develop questions in a variety of topics and to assess their own learning.

Procedure

Before reading, ask students to brainstorm what is known about a topic. They should categorize what is prior knowledge, predict or anticipate what the text might be about, and create questions to be answered. During reading, have the students refer to their questions and think of what might answer them. After reading, have the class discuss the information, write responses to their questions, and organize the information.

This strategy may be done on a sheet with three columns: Know, Want to Know, Learned. Guide the instruction the first few times it is used. Modeling is effective for the initial use.

Language Arts

Know	Want to Know	Learned
nouns	adverbs	modifies a verb, adjective, or another adverb
pronouns	prepositions	combines with noun, pronoun, or noun equivalent
verbs	proper punctuation	correct use of commas, colons, semicolons, quotation marks
adjectives		
capitalization		

Social Studies

Topic: Ancient Egypt

Know	Want to Know	Learned
pharaohs	Why did they mummify people?	believed in an afterlife
buried dead		
pyramid	How long did it take to build a pyramid?	sometimes a lifetime
mummified people		

(continued)

Banikowski & Mehring, 1999; Cantrell, 1997; Gunning, 1996; Ogle, 1986, 1994; Warren & Flynt, 1995

Science
Topic: Earthquakes

Know	*Want to Know*	*Learned*
shaking near coast a lot lately	What causes them?	shifting of rock
	Can you prevent them?	no, but you can build buildings to withstand it

Math
Topic: Adding Fractions

Know	*Want to Know*	*Learned*
adding with like denominators	adding with different denominators	find a common denominator, change fraction, then add
changing improper fractions to mixed fractions		

Assessment

Through comparison of the "Want to Know" column with the "Learned" column, class discussion, and a quiz or test, determine if students have learned the information they originally wanted to know more about. If there are still items they want to learn additional information about, discuss this with them. Ideally, each student should complete the "Learned" column with completed information about items in the "Want to Know" column along with new information they learned along the way.

Reflection

- Did students cover enough of the topic in their charts?
- How could you ensure that the most important aspects are included in this activity?
- What could you have done differently to make this activity more successful?
- What worked well?

Mapping

Mapping provides a visual guide for students to clarify textual information such as characters, setting, problems, reactions, and outcome. This strategy allows you to visually determine students' comprehension, and it provides students with a strategy that they can use on their own when they are dealing with other topics.

Procedure

Model an example of a map for students, talking through each step and having students assist in filling in the different areas. After comprehension of this strategy is assured, have students complete various maps on their own.

Language Arts
Characters: _____
Setting: Place _____ Time _____
Problem: _____
Events: _____
_____
_____
_____
Resolution: _____
Outcome: _____

Social Studies
Topic: Ancient Egypt

pharaohs	medicines	pyramids	afterlife	gods	mummification
___	___	___	___	___	___
___	___	___	___	___	___
___	___	___	___	___	___
___	___	___	___	___	___

Science
Topic: States of Matter
Solids: _____
Liquids: _____
Gases: _____

(continued)

Swanson & De La Paz, 1998; Vacca & Vacca, 1989; Vallecorsa & deBettencourt, 1997

Assessment

Evaluate students' maps to determine level of comprehension by the percentage of correct responses.

Reflection

- How much information should you provide to begin the activity?
- How would this work as an independent activity for students?
- What could you have done differently to make this activity more successful?
- What worked well?

Mind Mapping

Mind Mapping provides a structured outline that you create, but is used as a visual guide for students to introduce and improve comprehension of new material. Once students understand the strategy, they can create their own Mind Maps to use with a variety of topics.

Procedure

Review the passage to be covered and pull out vocabulary and key facts that are necessary for basic comprehension. Organize the information to show relationships and create a map using visual elements. Present the map to the class and have students discuss and contemplate meanings of new words and relationships. Next, have students use the Mind Map while reading a new selection. They can add pictures or words to the map, choose to highlight sections, create their own map, or use the original map to summarize the material.

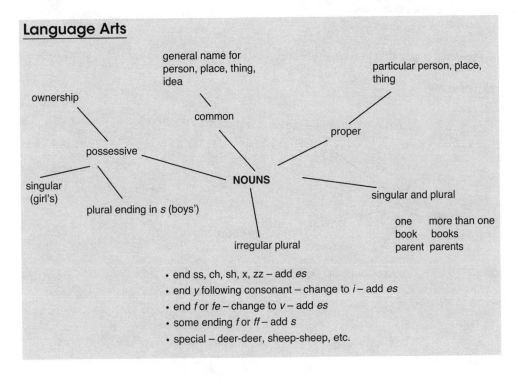

Language Arts

general name for person, place, thing, idea

particular person, place, thing

ownership

common

proper

possessive

NOUNS

singular (girl's)

plural ending in *s* (boys')

singular and plural

one — more than one
book — books
parent — parents

irregular plural

- end ss, ch, sh, x, zz – add *es*
- end *y* following consonant – change to *i* – add *es*
- end *f* or *fe* – change to *v* – add *es*
- some ending *f* or *ff* – add *s*
- special – deer-deer, sheep-sheep, etc.

(continued)

Barron, 1969; Buehl, 2009; Jonson, 2006; Tierney & Readence, 2004

Social Studies

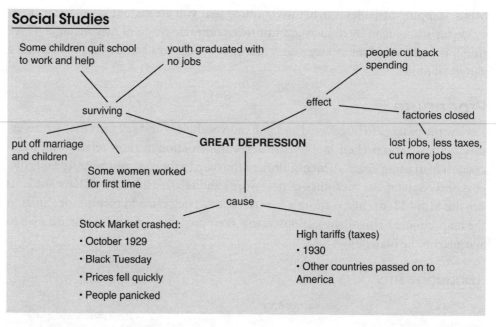

Some children quit school to work and help

youth graduated with no jobs

people cut back spending

effect

factories closed

surviving

GREAT DEPRESSION

lost jobs, less taxes, cut more jobs

put off marriage and children

Some women worked for first time

cause

Stock Market crashed:
• October 1929
• Black Tuesday
• Prices fell quickly
• People panicked

High tariffs (taxes)
• 1930
• Other countries passed on to America

Science

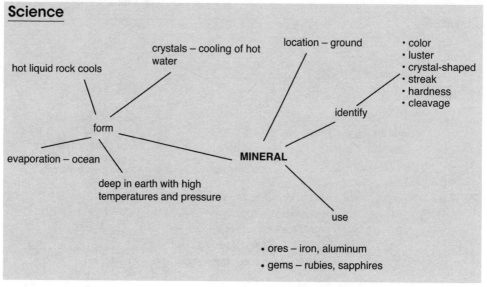

crystals – cooling of hot water

location – ground

• color
• luster
• crystal-shaped
• streak
• hardness
• cleavage

hot liquid rock cools

identify

form

MINERAL

evaporation – ocean

deep in earth with high temperatures and pressure

use

• ores – iron, aluminum
• gems – rubies, sapphires

Assessment

Evaluate students' maps to determine level of comprehension by asking questions and determining the percentage of correct responses and review the overall information provided.

Reflection

• Did your students' Mind Maps demonstrate understanding of the text?

• Was there important information that was left off of the Mind Map?

• Did the students adequately cover the topic?

• What could you have done differently to make this activity more successful?

• What worked well?

ORDER

This strategy can be used for a variety of subject areas to assist students in visually organizing and reviewing information. Once the strategy is learned, students can use it independently.

Procedure

First, instruct the class on the following steps in the strategy and assist them until they become familiar enough to use it on their own:

- [O]pen your mind and take notes.
- [R]ecognize the structure of the text.
- [D]raw an organizer—something visual (e.g., outline, map, chart).
- [E]xplain the organizer to others.
- [R]euse it as a study guide.

It is helpful to model this strategy several times and then have students assist in completing a visual organizer before they are required to do this on their own.

Language Arts
Parts of Speech Organizer

Article	Adjective	Noun	Adverb	Verb	Prepositional Phrase

Social Studies

Weather	*Climate*
day-to-day changes in the air temperature precipitation	average weather over many years

Science
States of Matter

Solids	
Liquids	
Gases	

Bulgren & Scanlon, 1998

Math

Converting Fractions to Decimals
1. Set up numerator divided by denominator.
2. Place decimal and add zero if needed.
3. Divide up to three places past the decimal.
4. Round to the nearest hundredth.

Assessment

Assess students' explanations of their organizers and evaluate the information included in the organizer to determine comprehension.

Reflection

• Were the organizers adequate to assist students in comprehending the text?

• Would it be possible to do this activity in groups?

• What could you have done differently to make this activity more successful?

• What worked well?

PLAN

This is a graphic organizer in which students create a map to visually organize and better understand the information that has been covered.

Procedure

There are four steps in this process:

- [P]redict the content or structure by using chapter titles and subheadings.
- [L]ocate known and unknown information. Students can indicate this by placing a ✓ by things they know and a ? by things they do not know.
- [A]dd words or phrases to the ? as students locate information about the topic.
- [N]ote new understanding of information and use it in instruction.

Language Arts

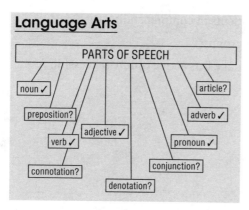

Social Studies

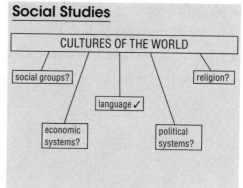

Science

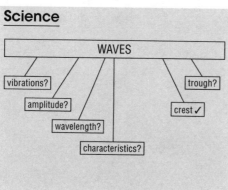

Math

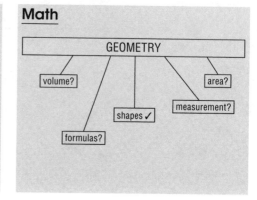

Caverly, Mandeville, & Nicholson, 1995; Vacca & Vacca, 1989

Assessment

Evaluate the answers that individual students provide to the questions in their organizer.

Reflection

- How could you help students add words or phrases to things they do not know?
- Would this work well in small groups?
- What could you have done differently to make this activity more successful?
- What worked well?

Pyramid Diagram

This strategy assists students in sorting through information in order to draw conclusions or make generalizations. It engages students in both reading and writing activities and can be used for a variety of subject areas. Once the strategy is learned, students can use it independently.

Procedure

Begin with a focusing question on a topic that helps students determine relevant information from a reading selection. Provide students with index cards to record information about the questions during reading. The cards are used in creating the visual of a pyramid. Show students how to categorize the information by grouping the cards together to form a foundation. Looking at the cards that can be grouped together, determine headings for each group. This creates the layer above the foundation. The next layer is a summary statement and the top layer is the title or topic. The students can then use all of the information to write a concluding paragraph.

Language Arts

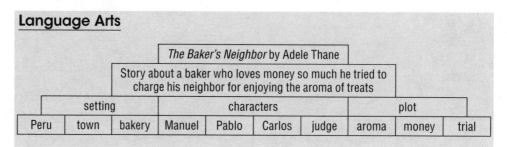

The Baker's Neighbor by Adele Thane

Story about a baker who loves money so much he tried to charge his neighbor for enjoying the aroma of treats

setting			characters				plot		
Peru	town	bakery	Manuel	Pablo	Carlos	judge	aroma	money	trial

Social Studies

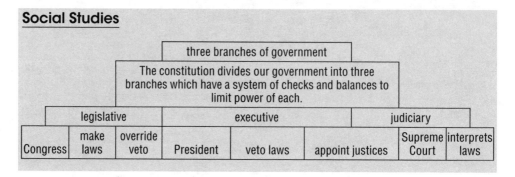

three branches of government

The constitution divides our government into three branches which have a system of checks and balances to limit power of each.

legislative			executive			judiciary		
Congress	make laws	override veto	President	veto laws	appoint justices	Supreme Court	interprets laws

Buehl, 2009; Solon, 1980

Science

			biomes			
		There are six major ecosystems on Earth called biomes. Some ways to identify them include climate and plants.				
taiga	deciduous forest	tropical rain forest	desert	tundra	grassland	
cold winter, cool summer, evergreens	mild summer, cold winter, hardwoods	hot year round, variety of plants	hot days, dry, few cacti, grasses	cold, nasty winter, grasses, mosses	cool winter, hot summer, grass, shrubs, some trees	

Math

			graphs						
		There are several types of graphs that can be used to display data.							
	pictograph			bar graph		line graph		circle graph	
symbols	pictures	key	horizontal or vertical	countable	data change over time	trends	good with %	parts to whole

Assessment

Assess students' explanations of their organizers and evaluate the information included in the organizer to determine comprehension.

Reflection

- Once students created all of the note cards, were they able to adequately categorize information and group cards together?
- What additional activities might you do to reinforce the skill of categorizing?
- What could you have done differently to make this activity more successful?
- What worked well?

Summary Cubes

Summary Cubes provide a structure for summarizing facts or displaying key points to assist in comprehension. Cubing allows students to look at six different aspects of a topic. The relationship of the topic to each side may vary.

Procedure

Summary Cubes help to retell key points of a text. Begin by explaining cubing and modeling for students. When assembled, the key points appear on a six-sided cube. Assist students in creating their own cubes based on the text. Share or display cubes.

Pattern:

Sample View:

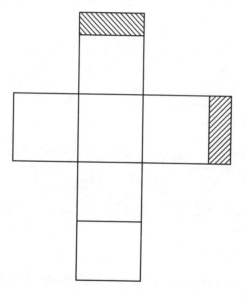

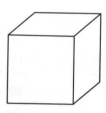

	Language Arts	Social Studies	Science	Math
Topic	*Casey at the Bat* by Ernest Lawrence Thayer	Egyptian Achievements	Animal Behavior	Shapes
Side 1	Title: *Casey at the Bat*	Writing: Hieroglyphics (symbols); papyrus (paper)	Behavior: Actions performed	Polyhedron

Jonson, 2006; McLaughlin & Allen, 2002; 2009

	Language Arts	Social Studies	Science	Math
Side 2	Type of Writing: Poem	Rosetta Stone: With Greek text, helped figure out hieroglyphics	Stimulus: Signal that causes an organism to react	Rectangular prism
Side 3	Style used: Hyperbole	Egyptian texts: Government records, historical, medical, literary	Response: Reaction to stimulus	Base – 1 rectangular base
Side 4	Sound devices: Rhyme, repetition, rhythm	Great Temples: Homes of gods, sphinxes, obelisks	Conditioning: Learning to connect stimulus with good or bad event	Face – 4 triangular faces
Side 5	Beginning: Hopeful	Paintings: Lively, colorful, heads and legs from side, bodies straight	Insight Learning: Solving a problem or learning to do something without trial and error	Vertices – 5 vertices
Side 6	Ending: Disappointed	Carvings/Jewelry: Skilled stoneworkers, gold and precious stones	Trial and Error Learning: Learning through repeated practice	Edges – 8 edges

Assessment

Assess students' explanations of their organizers and evaluate the information included in the organizer to determine comprehension.

Reflection

- Did your students demonstrate understanding of the text?
- Was the information on the sides relevant and informative?
- What are some ways to use summary cues to help students review information?
- What could you have done differently to make this activity more successful?
- What worked well?

Promoting Independent Learning

This section offers strategies that students can learn and apply independently in numerous situations. The main focus is teaching the necessary steps of each strategy so students are able to use a particular strategy independently when needed. These strategies provide students with a way to approach a particular concept, word, or section of text, or to question and break down the information into steps in order to increase their levels of understanding. Creating independent learners is the ultimate goal. Although it is important for students to know how to interact with others, it is also important for them to know, as individuals, strategies that can assist them in comprehending new material or extending learning of previously taught information.

CONCEPT

LANGUAGE ARTS

SOCIAL STUDIES

SCIENCE

This strategy clarifies and enhances information related to a single concept. The strategy is involved, but it is beneficial when you are beginning to teach a unit or concept that might be challenging for the students. It allows students to use the format provided to move ahead independently with their learning.

Procedure

This strategy involves the following steps:

- [C]onvey the concept to the students by naming the topic that is being studied.
- [O]ffer the overall concept by explaining what it is related to.
- [N]ote the keywords involved with the concept.
- [C]lassify characteristics about the topic.
- [E]xplore some examples and see if they fit the key concept definition.
- [P]ractice with new examples. (Give examples and assist the students to see if the new examples fit the key concept definition.)
- [T]ie down a definition.

Language Arts

Topic: Haiku
C—haiku
O—a Japanese poem
N—syllables
C—3 lines, 5-7-5 syllables
E—sunlight on the lake, glittering, shimmering bright, sparkles like the stars
P—Write various examples.
T—A haiku is a three-line Japanese form of poetry that (in general English form) is no more than 17 syllables and is usually in the 5-7-5 format.

Social Studies

Topic: Settlers
C—settlers
O—people in America
N—move, new (use prior knowledge and text)
C—Settlers move to an unfamiliar land, build permanent houses, bring their personal values.
E—Pioneers in 1800s American West? (yes) Native Americans in 1800s American West? (no)
P—Give examples of groups; students indicate if they meet the requirements of settlers.
T—For our purposes, settlers are people in America who have moved to an unfamiliar place, built permanent houses, and brought their own values to their new home.

(continued)

Bulgren & Scanlon, 1998

Science

Topic: Abiotic factors

C—abiotic factors
O—part of ecosystem
N—nonliving
C—survival, nonliving, photosynthesis, respiration, carbon dioxide
E—plants (no); water (yes); air (yes); soil (yes)
P—Give examples of groups; students indicate if they meet the requirements of abiotic factors.
T—Abiotic factors are nonliving parts of an ecosystem. These are needed in order for living things to survive.

Assessment

By discussing and checking the "P" (practice) and "T" (tying down a definition), determine if students clearly understand the concept.

Reflection

• Were your students able to complete all steps without prompting from you?

• What could you have done differently to make this activity more successful?

• What worked well?

DISSECT Word Identification Strategy

This strategy offers students several means to learn unfamiliar words.

Procedure

There are seven steps in this process; however, once the students understand the meaning of the word, it is not necessary to continue through the remaining steps:

- [D]iscover the word's context by using clues in the text.
- [I]solate the prefix and assess the meaning (skip if there is no prefix).
- [S]eparate the suffix (skip if there is no suffix).
- [S]ay the stem by reading the root.
- [E]xamine the stem by separating letters to make decoding easier.
- [C]heck with someone if necessary.
- [T]ry the dictionary if still having difficulties.

Language Arts
Word: *incomprehensible*
The steps would lead to the word *comprehend*. The definition of *understand* would be used. Finally, the definition "unable to understand" would be given for the original word.

Social Studies
Word: *inalienable*
The steps would lead to the word *alien*. The definition "belonging to another person" would be used. Finally, the definition "unable to transfer to another" would be given for the original word.

Science
Word: *unsaturated*
The steps would lead to the word *saturated*, then *saturate*. The definition "full of moisture" would be used. Finally, the definition "capable of absorbing" would be given for the original word.

Math
Word: *inequality*
The steps would lead to the word *equal*. The definition "identical in mathematical value" would be used. Finally, the definition "not the same value" would be given for the original word.

Assessment

Through your teacher questioning and discussion, determine if students are able to understand the meaning of the word and use it in context. Answering aloud regarding the word's definition can assist in this. Allow students to contribute their suggestions to the correct meaning of a word with your guidance. If necessary, refer students to one of the steps in the DISSECT strategy.

(continued)

Bryant, Ugel, Thompson, & Hamff, 1999

Reflection

- What support is needed for students to use this strategy?
- What could you have done differently to make this activity more successful?
- What worked well?

Narrow and Enlarge the Text

LANGUAGE ARTS

SOCIAL STUDIES

SCIENCE

MATH

This strategy is designed to help individual students by simplifying the amount of information that is covered. Although this strategy is not for everyone, it is helpful to the individual student whose reading level may be below grade level and who looks at text as overwhelming and difficult because of the small type and numerous words.

Procedure

Photocopy and enlarge sections of text to focus on the main points and important facts. Cut and place each concept on separate sheets of paper to assist students who have difficulties with text because they feel overwhelmed.

Language Arts
Choose a story or text selection. Copy and enlarge portions dealing with the main characters and events, and glue them on separate pages. Have students read and discuss main points, then students may choose to read the original text.

Social Studies/Science
Choose a section of text. Copy and enlarge vocabulary and main concepts and glue on separate pages. Have students read and discuss main points. Students may then choose to read the original text.

Math
With pages that have several problems, choose a few to copy, enlarge, and place on a separate page.

Assessment

Evaluate comprehension by discussing the main ideas and using written questions. Students should correctly respond to written or discussion questions.

Reflection

• Was the selection chosen adequate to ensure comprehension?

• Would it be possible for students to do this by themselves?

• What could you have done differently to make this activity more successful?

• What worked well?

Question–Answer Relationship

This strategy helps students to recognize the four possible areas in which answers can be found:

1. Right there—in a single sentence in the text.
2. Putting it together—in several sentences in the text.
3. On my own—in the student's background knowledge.
4. Writer and me—in a combination of information from text and reader's background.

Procedure

Have students read a story, text selection, or math problem. Use questions from the textbook or create questions on your own for students to answer. Determine what information is needed to answer each question. Decide if the information is "right there," stated plainly in one sentence in the text; if it requires reading several sentences to answer; if the answer is not in the text but can be answered using students' background information; or if it can be answered by combining background information with information from the text.

Language Arts
Topic: A Short Story
1. Right there: What is the setting?
2. Putting it together: Why was the character upset?
3. On my own: In what situations have you been upset?
4. Writer and me: Is there anyone who reminds you of the character in the story? Who and why?

Social Studies
Topic: Egyptian Religion
1. Right there: Who was the god of the living and dead?
2. Putting it together: What beliefs did people have about Amon-Re?
3. On my own: Why would religion be important to the people?
4. Writer and me: Why would Egyptians prepare so much for the afterlife?

Science
Topic: Erosion
1. Right there: What is erosion?
2. Putting it together: How is erosion related to weathering?
3. On my own: Have you experienced any difficulties dealing with erosion in your life?
4. Writer and me: What areas around you have problems with erosion and what can be done about it?

Banikowski & Mehring, 1999; Gunning, 1996; McIntosh & Draper, 1996;
Pearson & Johnson, 1978; Raphael, 1982; Swanson & De La Paz, 1998

Math

1. Right there: What is an integer?
2. Putting it together: What types of integers are there?
3. On my own: When would I use negative numbers?
4. Writer and me: How would I balance a checkbook?

Assessment

Check to see if correct responses are given for "Right there" and "Putting it together." If not, refer students back to the text. Use your evaluation to assess "On my own" and "Writer and me."

Reflection

• Do students need to do all four parts of this strategy to ensure comprehension?

• How could you assist students in connecting to background knowledge?

• What could you have done differently to make this activity more successful?

• What worked well?

Read Three Times

This is a mathematics strategy used in solving word problems and logic problems. The strength of this strategy is the specific steps used to assist students in determining what is necessary to solve the problem. Once students have used this strategy several times, they should be able to use it without referring to their notes.

Procedure

Students should begin by reading through a word problem quickly. Then they should list words they do not understand. Next, they need to answer the following questions:

- What is the problem asking you to do?
- What do you need to know?
- What is unnecessary information?
- What materials do you need?
- What math operation(s) will you use?

The students should read through the problem at least two more times until they understand. If they still have problems, they should ask for help.

> **Math**
>
> Problem: The temperature was recorded at 15 degrees C. It rose 8, fell 6, rose 12, and fell 23. What was the temperature after these changes?
> - What is the problem asking you to do? *Asking me to add and subtract to find final temperature.*
> - What do you need to know? *Need to know about integers.*
> - What is unnecessary information? *All information is necessary.*
> - What materials do you need? *No materials needed except paper and pencil.*
> - What math operation(s) will you use? *I will use + and – to solve.*

Assessment

Go through each of the questions in the procedure with the students and see if their responses and final answers are correct. If the answer is incorrect, review each step to determine where the error was made.

Manning, 1999b

Reflection

- How could you adapt this strategy to use with other topics?
- How might a graphic organizer with the questions be helpful to struggling students?
- What could you have done differently to make this activity more successful?
- What worked well?

SCAN and RUN

This strategy consists of seven cues for strategies that assist students in planning and monitoring comprehension before, during, and after reading. SCAN is used before reading and RUN is used during reading. Comprehension is extended after reading through discussion and answering questions.

Procedure

To begin, you must introduce, model, and help students to memorize the strategy. It is best to start with whole-group instruction. The steps for SCAN are as follows:

- [S]urvey Heading and Turn Them Into Questions (scan titles, headings, and subheadings and turn them into questions)
- [C]apture the Captions and Visuals (try to understand what each caption or visual clue means)
- [A]ttack Boldface Words (read highlighted words and figure out what they mean)
- [N]ote and Read the Chapter Questions (read questions at end of chapter before reading the selection)

The steps for RUN are as follows:

- [R]ead and Adjust Speed (change reading speed based on level of difficulty of the selection)
- [U]se Word Identification Skills Such as Sounding It Out, Looking for Other Word Clues in the Sentence, or Breaking Words Into Parts for Unknown Words (finding a way to identify unknown words that are difficult to pronounce)
- [N]otice and Check Parts You Don't Understand and Reread or Read On (place a check mark or use a sticky note when you do not understand something so you can come back to it)

Once the strategy has been modeled and students have an understanding of the steps, they can use it independently while reading a text. After reading, comprehension is extended through discussion and answering questions.

Salembier, 1999

Language Arts

Topic: Elaboration

S—What is elaboration? How do sensory details help with elaboration? How does adding facts enhance the story? How does creating visuals add to the story?

C—

TYPES OF ELABORATION
Sensory details
Facts
Visuals

A—elaborate, sensory details, facts

N—Elaborate on the following sentence: Having a younger sibling can make life difficult.

Social Studies

Topic: Canada

S—Describe Canada's landscape

C—(caption) Toronto and its suburbs have more than 4 million people, making it Canada's largest urban center.

A—Canadian shield, prairie, cordillera, newsprint

N—Name four minerals found in the Canadian shield. Explain why some Canadians worry about NAFTA.

Science

Topic: Air Pressure

S—What are the properties of air? How do you measure air pressure? How does the increasing altitude affect air pressure?

C—Density = Mass

A—density, pressure, air pressure, barometer

N—How does increasing the density of gases affect its pressure? Why is air at the top of a mountain hard to breathe?

(continued)

Math

Topic: Collecting and Displaying Data

S—How are tables used? What are mean, median, mode, and range?

C—

TIME	TEMPERATURE
6:00 a.m.	69°
10:00 a.m.	74°
2:00 p.m.	79°

A—bar graph, coordinate grid, ordered pair, range

N—Find the mean, median, mode, and range of the following:
Ages of students: 10, 11, 9, 11, 12, 10, 12, 9, 11, 13

Assessment

Through your teacher questioning and discussion, determine student level of comprehension of the text. If necessary, refer students to one of the steps in the SCAN and RUN strategy.

Reflection

- What word identification skills might students need to assist them in understanding the text?
- Did students adjust their speed of reading as needed?
- What could you have done differently to make this activity more successful?
- What worked well?

SQ3R

Although this strategy takes time, it is very effective in improving comprehension because students are allowed to break text into manageable parts.

Procedure

Begin by teaching students the following steps:

- [S]urvey—Look through the chapter that is going to be studied for an overall idea of the topic.
- [Q]uestion—Turn each heading into a question.
- [R]ead to answer the questions.
- [R]ecite—At the end of each section, try to answer the questions without looking back; do not take notes until the entire section is read.
- [R]eview what you have read; go over all the questions you asked yourself and try to answer them.

Modeling a previously studied chapter helps students to understand the steps. This is a strategy they can use independently in the future.

Social Studies	Science
S—Egypt's Powerful Kings and Queens Q—Who were Egypt's God-Kings and why were they called that? How did Egypt remain in power for 2,000 years? Who was the Powerful Queen, Great Pharaoh? Read - Recite answers – Review	S—Moving Water Q—How do the earth's surfaces affect what happens to water? How does water cycle through the environment? What happens to rainwater that runs off? How can the water level in the ground be changed? Read - Recite answers - Review

Assessment

Determine student comprehension through evaluation of the questions used for headings, correct answers given, discussion, and your observation. Your observation should include monitoring the involvement of individual students and their responses. Discussion can be used to determine students' level of comprehension by assessing their responses during the "recite" and "review" parts of the strategy.

(continued)

Gunning, 1996; Jonson, 2006; Robinson, 1961

Reflection

- What guidance did your students need to complete this strategy?
- What additional modeling might be necessary to aid students in this strategy?
- What could you have done differently to make this activity more successful?
- What worked well?

Teaching Vocabulary

LANGUAGE ARTS

SOCIAL STUDIES

SCIENCE

Rather than having students write out vocabulary words and define them using a dictionary, students use the context of the literature they are reading to figure out a word's meaning. This strategy can begin as a class activity by writing unknown words on the chalkboard and going through the procedures as a group. Eventually, students should be able to create individual lists and follow the procedures on their own.

Procedure

First, students should look through a story or text section and underline or write down unknown words. Next they should predict what they believe to be the meaning of each word based on the context. Finally, discuss these words as a group to determine meaning.

Language Arts
Word: *presumptuous*
Sentence: *She was presumptuous because she said she already had a frame for the winning certificate.*
Predicted meaning: confident, bold

Social Studies
Word: *quarantined*
Sentence: *The immigrants with diseases were quarantined until they were no longer contagious.*
Predicted meaning: kept by themselves

Science
Word: *unsaturated*
Sentence: *The sponge was unsaturated so it was used to clean up the spill.*
Predicted meaning: able to absorb liquid

Assessment

Review predicted meanings. Discussion can be used to determine students' level of comprehension by assessing their responses after reading.

Reflection

- When should you allow students to use a dictionary?
- How do you guide students in the right direction?
- What could you have done differently to make this activity more successful?
- What worked well?

Dole, Sloan, & Trathen, 1995

Text Lookbacks

Often, students feel they are not allowed to use their textbooks for studying. Instead, students rely on their notes. They need to realize that the textbook is a study guide, and it should be used to clarify or locate information when studying. Once the students have learned this strategy, they can use it on their own.

Procedure

Discuss with students that it is appropriate during studying to "look back" through the textbook to locate information. Begin by modeling skimming for information with the students. It is helpful to begin with short passages and to proceed to longer ones. Explain how to use headings and boldfaced words to search for information.

Language Arts/Social Studies/ Science
Use the strategy with short sections of text that have questions at the end.

Math
Use the strategy throughout a textbook to review proper operations or necessary information.

Assessment

Answers given to the questions orally or in writing help determine students' level of comprehension.

Reflection

• Were your students able to use this strategy without prompting once you modeled it?

• How could you encourage students to refer to the textbook?

• What could you have done differently to make this activity more successful?

• What worked well?

Swanson & De La Paz, 1998

Thick and Thin Questions

This strategy is designed to help individual students create questions about the text, learn about levels of questioning, and use questions to gain the ability to facilitate understanding of the text. To begin, students learn the strategy in a group or paired setting. They may then use it independently.

Procedure

Discuss the differences in thick and thin questions. Thin questions deal with specific content or words. They usually require short answers and are close ended. Thick questions are more involved, complex, and open ended. Thick questions require higher order thinking. Guide students to work with partners to create thick and thin questions. Share the questions and answers in small and large groups. Once this strategy is understood, students may use it independently in their reading.

Language Arts
Topic: *Anne Frank: The Diary of a Young Girl* **by Anne Frank**
Thick
Why were the Jews hated so much? How can some people think it is fine to exterminate a group of people?
Thin
Who helped to protect Anne Frank? Why were they in hiding?

Social Studies
Topic: The Origin of Judaism
Thick
Why was the Exodus significant to Jewish history? How do you think celebrating traditions and holy days help Jews connect to their past?
Thin
Who first led the Jews to Canaan? What is monotheism?

Science
Topic: Animal Behavior
Thick
How is animal behavior similar to human behavior? If the first thing a duck saw after birth was a cat walking by, what would happen the next time the duck sees a cat walking by?
Thin
What is imprinting? What are the functions of most animal behavior?

(continued)

Buehl, 2009; Lewin & Shoemaker, 1998

Assessment

Evaluate comprehension by correct responses to both thick and thin questions. Assess students' ability to tell the difference between thick and thin questions. Have students generate their own thick and thin questions to solidify and demonstrate understanding of the concept.

Reflection

- Did the thick questions add to students' level of comprehension?
- How could you get students to ask more thick questions when they are reading independently?
- What could you have done differently to make this activity more successful?
- What worked well?

Think-Aloud

Think-Aloud can help students to understand the thought processes associated with silent reading. This strategy helps students recognize that they should be thinking about various things related to the text as they read. Students may then be encouraged to use this strategy on their own.

Procedure

Model this strategy by reading a short selection aloud. Students should talk about their thoughts regarding the selection by discussing what they understand and what they may need to learn more about.

Language Arts
While reading a story, ask questions such as Why is this character acting as he or she is? What may have happened to cause this character to be in this place at this time? What would you do? When and where does the story take place?

Social Studies
While reading about Egypt's kings and queens, ask questions such as How did they know the statues that appeared to be men were actually of women?

Assessment

Use discussion, tests, quizzes, and your teacher questioning. Discussion can be used to determine student's level of comprehension by assessing their responses after reading. Encourage responses from students who appear off task. Students should correctly respond to questions during a discussion or those given on a quiz or test.

Reflection

- Would it be possible to let students work in groups and have a leader model the strategy?
- How could you ensure this would be effective?
- What could you have done differently to make this activity more successful?
- What worked well?

Gunning, 1996

Vocabulary Notebooks

This strategy requires that students keep a notebook with vocabulary words from the text and words that you assigned. Students look up the words in a dictionary or are given definitions, and then they write an original sentence using each word. Having the students create their own sentences rather than copying sentences with the vocabulary words ensures that they understand the meaning of each word. This should enhance students' text comprehension by providing a resource for understanding unfamiliar words.

Procedure

Have the students keep a notebook for your class. As you introduce new topics, write vocabulary words on the board and have students copy them in their notebooks. You can give students the definitions or have them look the words up in a glossary or dictionary. Have students use each word in a sentence. If students find additional words they do not know, have them add the words to their vocabulary notebook. The notebooks will be valuable tools as students read and study.

Language Arts
Use with vocabulary from stories and adapt as a grammar notebook (e.g., *preposterous*, *magnanimous*). Use vocabulary words from the text or create a list of your own.

Social Studies
Use with vocabulary words such as *irrigation*, *terrain*, *constitution*, *latitude*, and *longitude*.

Science
Use with vocabulary such as *lunar*, *constellation*, and *biology*.

Math
Use with mathematical terms such as *proportion*, *parallel*, and *quadrilateral*.

Assessment

Use your teacher questioning, discussion, and student responses to show understanding of the words. Your questioning should involve individual student responses to check for understanding. Discussion can be used to determine students' level of comprehension by assessing their responses to the vocabulary terms.

Bean & Zigmond, 1994

Reflection

- Did your students cover all of the necessary vocabulary?
- How could you encourage students to choose their own vocabulary to add to their list?
- What could you have done differently to make this activity more successful?
- What worked well?

Teaching to Learning Style

This section contains strategies that specifically focus on one or more modes of learning (e.g., visual, auditory, tactile). Because students learn in a variety of ways, you can use these strategies to help students with particular learning styles who have strength in a certain modality. There are many ways to determine a student's particular learning style or strength. It can be done through a formal assessment (many of which are available through the Internet or through a variety of companies), individual assessments (some of which are formal and some of which are informal), or observation in the classroom to determine which learning style tends to help students succeed.

Audiotapes/CDs

LANGUAGE ARTS

SOCIAL STUDIES

SCIENCE

MATH

Using audiotapes or CDs improves text comprehension for students who have difficulty reading and for students who better comprehend information obtained through auditory means. The strategy allows students individually and in small groups to listen to information several times until they have comprehended the material. This is a strategy that is most useful in areas in which there are long passages of text such as in literature, science, and social studies.

Procedure

Use tapes or CDs that have been provided with the text, or have volunteers read and record the text. These can be used with the entire class or with individual students who use headphones during silent reading. Individual students also could check tapes or CDs out or use them at a time outside class. The use of adjustable speed recorders is beneficial with tapes because readers may slow the tape if the reader is reading too fast.

Language Arts

Use the strategy primarily with stories and poems. If volunteers are recording, ask them to read with expression, and to read any questions that might be associated with the text. This also can be used to reinforce grammar skills by reading over the grammar/usage rules and giving examples on tapes or CDs.

Social Studies/Science

Use with any text that might benefit the student. It is best to use short tapes and record each section or chapter on a separate tape or divide the CD into tracks. Have these available prior to the lesson so students are able to go over the text before it is used in class.

Math

Use with word problems. Additional information can be given on the tape or CD to assist students in choosing the correct method for solving the problems.

Assessment

Determine from your questioning, text questions, and discussion whether the student is comprehending the text. Your questioning and text questions should assist in determining student comprehension. Students should correctly respond to the questions. Discussion can be used to determine students' comprehension by assessing their responses after reading.

(continued)

Koskinen, 1995

Reflection

- Were your students able to gain adequate comprehension from this strategy?
- How could this be used with small groups?
- Would it be helpful to have students make recordings?
- What could you have done differently to make this activity more successful?
- What worked well?

Combined Reading

Combined reading gives students the opportunity to receive information in both visual (silent reading) and auditory (reading aloud) modalities.

Procedure

First, assign a passage for silent reading. After a sufficient amount of time, instruct the students to begin reading aloud in a specific arrangement. This may involve students reading aloud in small groups, individuals reading in a group setting, or you modeling reading aloud. Tactile learners may be instructed to use a bookmark to follow along with the reading of the text.

Language Arts
Topic: Poem
After students have read the poem silently, assign partners to alternate reading lines or verses to each other. Regroup and discuss the poem with the whole class.

Social Studies
Topic: Egyptian Pyramids
After silent reading, reread the selection by calling on individual students randomly. At the end of the selection, discuss and ask questions.

Science
Topic: Cells
After reading silently, divide the class into four groups. Assign a strong reader in each group and have each reader read aloud to his or her group. Allow time for small-group discussion before bringing the class together.

Assessment

Through discussion and your teacher questioning, determine the level of comprehension from the group. Individuals may be regrouped and allowed to reread as necessary. Your questioning should involve individual student responses to check for understanding. Discussion can be used to determine students' level of comprehension by assessing their responses. If students do not answer correctly, refer them to the text.

(continued)

Bean & Zigmond, 1994

Reflection

• Were your students able to gain adequate comprehension from this strategy?
• Did you group students appropriately to maximize their comprehension?
• What could you have done differently to make this activity more successful?
• What worked well?

Creative Dramatics

This strategy is a creative, exciting way to motivate students while using kinesthetic movement in helping them focus on the main idea they are studying. The strategy is an interesting way for students to understand why a character may act a certain way, and it can be used with a variety of situations.

Procedure

Decide what main point you would like to cover. This may be related to character or historical motivation or actions. Before introducing the reading, present situations to the students that they are familiar with and that are related to the main point of the reading.

Choose students to participate in acting out the situation and have them make decisions regarding what they would do. Assist students as necessary as they prepare the "acting" situation. Guide students by presenting questions that lead them to realize why a person might respond in a certain way. After this has been done, students read the story or text and discuss the relationship between the creative drama activity and the reading.

Language Arts

Topic: Julius Caesar
Ask three students to role-play. One would be the new school president; the other two would be his or her friends who are unsure of the way the president is using his or her power. One friend would be afraid that the school would suffer because of the president's abuse of power. Ask the students to decide what they would do, including what action would be taken if the president refused to listen to their concerns.

Assessment

Through discussion, your observation, and questioning, determine if students are able to state the main idea in the lesson they are covering. Your observation should include monitoring the involvement of individual students and their responses. Your questioning and discussion can be used to determine students' level of comprehension by assessing their responses. Encourage responses from students who appear off task. If students do not respond correctly, provide additional information and refer them to the text to reexamine the passage.

Kaplan, 1997

(continued)

Reflection

- How could you ensure that all students are involved—even those who do not feel comfortable performing?
- Did you choose ideas that represented the text well?
- What could you have done differently to make this activity more successful?
- What worked well?

Draw a Picture

This strategy is simple, yet gives a way for students to be successful. Because many students learn visually, this strategy helps them to organize and conceptualize what a text is about. It is also advantageous for tactile learners.

Procedure

After students have read a story or passage, ask them to draw a simple picture of what the text is about. Explain to them that stick figures are acceptable. Give guidelines for the pictures by having students answer the following questions in their drawings: What is the setting? Who are the characters? When did the story take place? What is happening?

If vocabulary is a problem, the students may label items or actions in the picture. After students have drawn their pictures, they should write a short summary paragraph. The short paragraph allows you to see if the student really understands the text.

Language Arts

Read a short story and ask students to think about setting, character, and events. Have them picture a scene in their mind that tells about the story. Ask students to draw a picture (stick figures are fine), label it, and write a summary paragraph. For example, students could illustrate a story about a girl who is always on the phone, so her parents limit her to three calls at three minutes each day. She is angry until a boy calls to ask her out and she realizes that he had been trying to call her for weeks, but the phone was always busy.

Social Studies

For example, in social studies, students could depict the unique aspects of life in Egypt: the gods they worshipped, belief in life after death, the pharaohs who ruled the country, and the workers who spent their lives building pyramids and other things for their leaders.

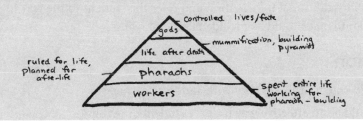

(continued)

Banikowski & Mehring, 1999; J. Pederson (personal communication, October 23, 1999)

Science

Read a short selection and ask students to think about the information presented. Have them picture a scene in their mind that tells about the selection. Ask students to draw a picture (stick figures are fine), label it, and write a summary paragraph. In science, students could depict the three states of matter: solids, liquids, and gases. Each of these has their own properties.

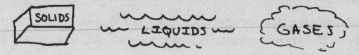

Math

Students could visually represent a word problem. For example, a boy purchases three drinks at $.90 each and two large popcorns at $1.25 each. He divides the total cost with his two friends. How much will each of the three have to pay?

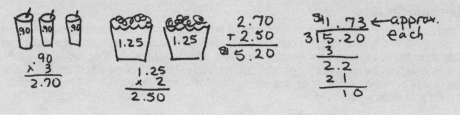

Assessment

Use your teacher evaluation of the drawing, evaluation of summary paragraph, and discussion to determine if the main ideas have been addressed. Your evaluation should include reviewing drawings with students to see if the drawings correctly conceptualize what the text is about. Discussion can be used to determine students' level of comprehension by assessing their responses. If the drawing does not represent the text correctly, provide additional information and refer the student to the text to reexamine the information that should be included in the drawing.

Reflection

• How could you use this strategy with auditory learners?

• What would be an effective way to share student drawings?

• What could you have done differently to make this activity more successful?

• What worked well?

Highlight Text

LANGUAGE ARTS

SOCIAL STUDIES

SCIENCE

MATH

This strategy helps students focus on the important points or items in a text. The highlighter colors help visual learners notice facts and important points in a text.

Procedure

Set a certain number of textbooks aside for students who need assistance identifying the important points or items in a text. The teacher or students, or both, review these texts with a highlighter to identify important information.

Language Arts
Use the strategy with stories, poems, or grammar; highlight main ideas, characters, and vocabulary.

Social Studies/Science
Use with any section of text; highlight vocabulary terms, names, places, and main concepts.

Math
Highlight words that identify which operation to use in solving a problem.

Assessment

Use your teacher evaluation, discussion, and a quiz or test to determine comprehension. Your observation should include monitoring the involvement of individual students and their responses. Discussion can be used to determine students' level of comprehension by assessing their responses after reading. Encourage responses from students who appear off task. Students should correctly respond to the questions during a discussion or given on a quiz. Assist students who need to continue to read aloud by pairing them with other readers.

Reflection

- Were your students able to gain adequate comprehension from this strategy?
- Did students choose appropriate words or phrases to highlight?
- Would tabs be as effective?
- What could you have done differently to make this activity more successful?
- What worked well?

Small, 1996

LANGUAGE ARTS

SOCIAL STUDIES

SCIENCE

MATH

Journal

This strategy is helpful in assessing comprehension and allowing students to think through the information that has been taught. It is most effective for tactile learners who tend to best sort information when it is written out. This is also useful in getting students to think about a theme such as "Life is not fair—agree or disagree" before reading Steinbeck's *The Red Pony*.

Procedure

The first step in this strategy involves giving a prompt that is instructional, contextual, reflective, or other. For example, when studying Egypt, ask the students, What type of person would you have wanted to be if you had lived in Ancient Egypt? Allow the students 5 to 8 minutes to write about the prompt. Students turn in their journals, and you are able to determine if their responses show comprehension of the material that was covered.

Language Arts
Ask students, What is the setting in this story? Which feelings is the main character expressing? How would you react in this situation?

Social Studies
Ask students, What type of person would you like to be if you had lived in Ancient Egypt? Why?

Science
Ask students, How are sounds produced? How do stirring and temperature affect dissolving?

Math
Ask, How would you tell someone to solve the following problem: $3x + 4x = 35$?

Assessment

Use your teacher observation and individual evaluation (written or oral) to determine if students are comprehending the text. Student writing should show a clear understanding of the main ideas.

Reflection

- How often should you collect journals?
- Would it be possible and effective to have peers review one another's journals?
- What could you have done differently to make this activity more successful?
- What worked well?

DiPillo & Sovchik, 1997; Vacca & Vacca, 1989

Magazine Covers to Summarize

LANGUAGE ARTS

SOCIAL STUDIES

SCIENCE

MATH

This strategy is effective with middle-grade learners because of their interest in magazines and related publications. Creating a magazine cover requires students to identify the important ideas in a text, capture the theme, and effectively summarize. The use of technology with this strategy allows students to integrate visual images and graphics with the details and key phrases from the text. When readers actively relate ideas represented in print to their own knowledge and experiences and create visual representations to make meaning, comprehension is enhanced. This is a motivating instructional strategy that can help students to take meaning beyond the written word and summarize the overall meaning of the text.

Procedure

There are four primary steps involved with this strategy. First, bring in age-appropriate magazines for the class to review and ask them to review the layouts, graphics, fonts, and headings. Second, students discuss how these elements provide important information. This can be done in small groups. Third, students should identify recurring topics or patterns in the headings and visual images and discuss how they support the overall purpose of the magazine. As they discuss and explain their thoughts, they must be able to support their ideas by using the magazines. Fourth, after students have practiced summarizing a text and have explored various magazine covers, they are then ready to create their own magazine cover using the computer to summarize the information.

This process may be done over time while other summarizing or comprehending activities are taking place. For students who may be overwhelmed with the amount of images and information on the Internet, you may create a folder with a limited number of available images. When students are finished, they may share with one another.

Language Arts
Students create a cover depicting the problem or outcome of a story. Headlines should indicate key points. The illustration should depict the main character or main event.

Social Studies
Students create a cover that depicts a major event in U.S. history such as the Gettysburg Address. Headlines should include major views of the time. The illustration should include something that shows the importance of the address.

Assaf & Garza, 2007; National Institute of Child Health and Human Development, 2000

(continued)

Science

Students create a cover that depicts a concept such as animal adaptations. Headlines should include why adaptations are important to animals. The illustration should include an example of an animal adaptation.

Math

Students create a cover depicting a concept such as volume of a cylinder. Headlines should include the formula and uses of volume. The illustration should include a sample of an item where cylindrical volume would be used.

Assessment

Review the student covers to determine the level of comprehension. Students should adequately convey the main idea and supporting ideas on the cover. It should be evident from the information chosen that the material is fully comprehended.

Reflection

- Did students choose appropriate words, phrases, ideas, and concepts to use as headlines?
- Was the illustration appropriate to show the main idea?
- What could you have done differently to make this activity more successful?
- What worked well?

Radio Reading

LANGUAGE ARTS

SOCIAL STUDIES

SCIENCE

MATH

This strategy is a simple form of oral reading that gives students many ways to learn information. Students are exposed to visual, auditory, and tactile learning.

Procedure

After students have read a selection independently, have individual students reread sections aloud. Students who are not reading aloud close their books and listen to the reader, concentrating on meaning. Afterward, students summarize the text, referring to the text if necessary.

Language Arts
Use the strategy with stories, poems, or text selections. Assign students to read specific passages and have their place marked so they are prepared when it is their turn.

Social Studies/Science
Use with text selections. It is preferable to have one student read through an entire selection before changing students.

Math
Use with word problems.

Assessment

Using discussion and student summaries, determine if students have comprehended the overall concept of the material. Discussion and student summaries can be used to determine students' level of comprehension by assessing their responses after reading. Students' responses should communicate the main idea of the text. If they do not, refer them to the text or have other students share their summaries.

Reflection

- Were your students engaged while listening?
- Did you choose readers who read well enough that it did not distract from the text?
- What could you have done differently to make this activity more successful?
- What worked well?

Vacca & Vacca, 1989

Visual Adjuncts

Often, visual adjuncts to text are overlooked, and student comprehension of these visuals is assumed when it should not be. These resources are particularly helpful for visual learners in helping to clarify concepts that are being studied.

Procedure

During text instruction, discuss in detail the tables, charts, graphs, and photos to assist students in clarifying, enriching, or reinforcing concepts that are discussed in the text. When appropriate, students can construct their own visuals to assist with comprehension.

Language Arts

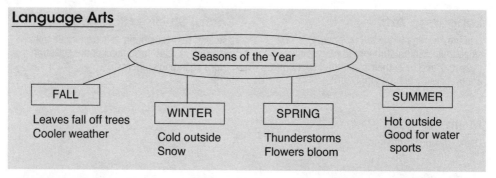

Social Studies

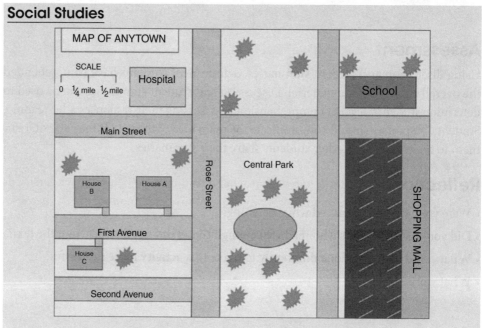

Craig & Yore, 1996

Science

Solid	Liquid	Gas
Ice	Water	Steam
Book	Peroxide	Carbon Monoxide
Pencil	Alcohol	Oxygen

Math

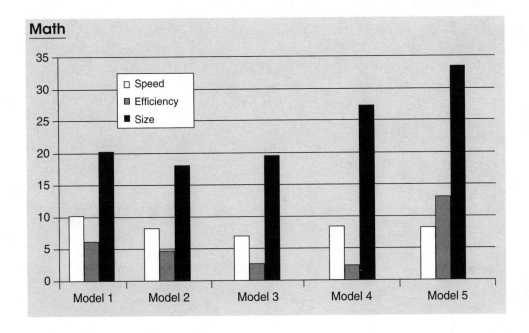

Assessment

Use discussion, quizzes, tests, and your teacher questioning to determine understanding of the visual adjuncts. Your observation should include monitoring the involvement of individual students and their responses. Discussion can be used to determine students' level of comprehension by assessing their responses after reading. Students should correctly respond to the questions posed in a discussion or given on a quiz.

(continued)

Reflection

- Would it be effective to have students create their own visuals when they are not available in the text?
- Would it be effective to have students use visuals that are in the text and adapt them to visually represent the material in an alternate manner?
- What could you have done differently to make this activity more successful?
- What worked well?

Technology and Comprehension

This section addresses technology and its possible uses for reading comprehension. Rather than describing a specific procedure and examples, this section contains an assortment of available technology and discussions as to how each may be used to assist with reading in the content areas. Technology continues to be available—and is actually necessary—in a variety of settings in our world. Because it has become more and more a part of our everyday lives, it is important for us to incorporate what is available to assist our students in whatever ways possible. Using technology in the classroom to aid in comprehension not only helps to increase student understanding but also increases knowledge regarding the various tools that are available, many of which can be transferred to other applications and uses in both educational and vocational settings.

Blogs and Wikis

A blog is a type of interactive website that allows posting of comments related to specific topics. Teachers can use blogs that are secure and only post items from students that have been previewed and approved. Blogs can be useful in allowing students to post responses to comprehension questions or to share their views and opinions about specific assignments. Students are then able to comment on the postings of other students. You can determine a student's understanding of a text by examining the content of his or her posts.

A wiki is a website that allows for editing, writing, and saving so each student that visits the site can make changes. It provides links to additional pages or websites. A wiki can allow students to concentrate on a specific topic or story and address key components to demonstrate comprehension.

CD-ROM Books

CD-ROM books allow students to have multisensory experiences such as audio, definitions, and graphics. These books may allow students to concentrate more on meaning and less on decoding and, therefore, may enhance comprehension for students who struggle with the reading process. Students may be assigned books that are appropriate to their individual level. It is important, however, that students do not rely on features from a CD-ROM as with other types of technology or they may not develop the necessary skills to make connections on their own.

CD-ROMs can be highly interactive and can lead to increased student engagement. In addition, they allow for self-pacing and address all three learning styles (i.e., visual, auditory, kinesthetic). Although it is not recommended that they be used in isolation, CD-ROM books can definitely enhance the reading and learning experience.

Pearman, 2008b

Computer Software

One of the greatest potential benefits of computer-based instructional products is to help differentiate instruction. There are many reading software programs that allow students to progress at their own rate. Some of these assess students to find their current reading level and then provide lessons to help them build on their current knowledge. When students are not successful, the software is designed to give remedial activities until the readers are able to proceed. When students are successful, the software is designed to move them forward at a faster pace.

There are also many computer programs available to students that can aid in demonstrating comprehension. This can be done by providing activities that are engaging and allowing students to show understanding of a topic in a variety of ways. After researching and reading information, students can use the information gained, along with certain software programs, to demonstrate comprehension. Students may use publishing programs to write essays, create brochures, and write newsletters. Presentation programs allow students to prepare information to share with the class or with you both in text and video formats. Many programs assist students by automatically checking grammar and spelling when writing, allowing them to focus more on the content.

Software programs that are beneficial for student use in the classroom include SuccessMaker, Super Source, HyperSnap, Inspiration 7, Mimio Notebook, SMART Notebook, Senteo, SMART Response, Microsoft Office PowerPoint, Microsoft Office Word, Microsoft Office Excel, Microsoft Publisher, Windows Movie Maker, Windows Media Audio, Switch Sound File Converter, Sound Recorder, Adobe Acrobat 8, Boardmaker, and Corel Photo Editor.

Pearman, 2008a

Digital Language Experience Approach (D-LEA)

The Digital Language Experience Approach, or D-LEA, allows students to sequence events, generate high oral language, and use highly descriptive vocabulary when using digital photos and arranging them in presentation software. A creative aspect of this strategy is that students are able to take the original information and transform it. This strategy has been shown to be effective with readers of all ages and has the potential to be very effective with middle school students. However, this strategy can be adapted for a variety of purposes and can be used with students at various levels.

There are four key steps in D-LEA. First, the experience is set up—preparing what will be done, where, and for how long. This could involve a content area concept such as an event in history or a section from a story or poem. Second, photographs are taken. Decide if the photos will be candid or posed, how many will be taken, and who will be the photographer. The photos should show meaning of the text that was read through visuals. Third, a multimedia story or photo essay is composed. Students can use a variety of software. To do this, they need to look through the photos and choose which ones to use, and then determine the sequence of the photos. They create a storyboard or production that shows understanding of the original experience. Fourth, students engage in follow-up activities. These may include individual reading, paired readings, and choral readings.

Labbo, Eakle, & Montero, 2002

Digital Photography and Flip Cameras

Digital cameras are relatively easy to use and allow students to produce pictures, videos, or both. Although the D-LEA describes only one activity, digital cameras can be used in an assortment of ways. Comprehension can be shown through projects and displays. For example, you can have groups of students review parts of a story and choose 10–15 key points for them to act out while you take still photos to print out and mix up. Students review the pictures, determine the order, and write captions. This demonstrates understanding of the key points in the story. They may also draw some pictures that can be scanned to be used in a presentation.

Flip cameras can be used to create videos that can then be used in a variety of computer programs such as Windows Movie Maker. Students may use the videos to demonstrate comprehension through various creations including scenes from a story, interviews, or documentaries.

K.R. McKenzie (personal communication, June 27, 2010)

e-Reader/e-Book/iPad

An e-reader, or electronic reader, is a handheld device that can be used to download reading content, such as e-books, newspapers, and documents. Stand-alone devices can be used to access the Internet to obtain additional information.

Examples of e-readers include Amazon's Kindle, Barnes and Noble's Nook, and Sony's Reader. Apple's iPad tablet also has the capability to download reading content. These devices are convenient for students to carry and allow them to look up unfamiliar words or concepts in the text. They also allow the content to be frequently updated. For these reasons, it is possible that e-readers may eventually replace textbooks.

Glogsters

Glogster.com is a social network that allows students to create interactive posters, or glogs (graphical blogs). The student creates a multimedia glog using text, clip art, images, photos, audio in MP3 format, videos, special effects, and other elements. They can create a glog about a specific topic or story. You can then view these glogs to assess comprehension, and they can be used by other students as additional study guides.

Interactive Whiteboards

Interactive whiteboards offer a large presentation space that can be viewed by all students. Many are operated by touch or with a stylus. The whiteboard can accommodate a variety of learning styles—especially for visual and tactile learners. One important benefit of using the interactive whiteboard is that students become engaged and motivated as they interact with the instruction. It is an effective tool to use with vocabulary and comprehension skills.

There are a variety of interactive whiteboards available, such as SMART boards, Promethean boards, and Mimios (which transform a regular dry-erase board into an interactive whiteboard). There are also low-cost ways to create your own interactive whiteboards. Once teachers have used the boards and realized the implications, it becomes a part of the daily routine for many. There are lessons that are already prepared and available through software and web-based sites. These are directed at specific lessons or skills. Many of the lessons involve reading and comprehension skills and can be used in conjunction with other sources or print materials.

Labbo, Love, & Ryan, 2007

The Internet

The Internet is no longer used primarily for leisure activities with adolescents; therefore, reading online is a skill students need to develop to do research in the middle grades and beyond. There are differences in reading print and hypertext. On the Internet, there are a greater number of pages, varieties of text, abundant sources, and varied quality of information. There are also links to other sources that can take you far away from your original search. Because of this, students need to know how to "bookmark" important pages for easy return. Students must also be taught to evaluate the information to determine the accuracy and quality. Just because something is available on the Internet does not mean it is valid or accurate. Further security and monitoring of Internet usage are essential.

To be successful using the Internet, readers must be able to manage the volume of text and numerous sites related to a topic, evaluate the features on the page and decide which is most appropriate, and be able to read expository text (which requires being familiar with concepts, vocabulary, and organizational format). Although the Internet is an ever-changing tool that can be used with reading, students must be taught the skills to both navigate through Internet text and apply knowledge about the reading process. This can best be done through modeling and instruction.

Leu, 2000; Malloy & Gambrell, 2006; Schmar-Doblar, 2003

iREAP

iREAP connects the Internet and the REAP system (Read, Encode, Annotate, Ponder), which has been in existence for years. REAP started as a way to improve content area reading and writing in urban schools. It helps students to think precisely and deeply by using the following steps:

1. Read to get the basic message
2. Encode the message into your own words
3. Annotate by writing responses from several perspectives
4. Ponder by reviewing, sharing, and discussing with others

The goal of REAP is to make it a habit to think from different perspectives. iREAP adds the Internet toward this end in ways such as teachers saving and building a collection of annotations, posting annotations to a webpage, linking webpages of several schools, having online instructional interactions, or partnering with a bookstore or organization in the community where communication could take place via the Web.

iREAP should lead to an increase and improvement in higher order thinking, reading comprehension, writing ability, content knowledge, and to building a shared experience of being a part of a community that is focused on a higher purpose.

Manzo, Manzo, & Albee, 2002

Student Response Systems

Student response systems can truly transform the content area classroom and can enhance your ability to have immediate feedback regarding content, comprehension, and application. These systems allow each student to have a "clicker" to respond to your questions. The answers may be multiple choice or open ended. You can see within a few seconds how students responded as a class or as individuals. The information can then be sent to a spreadsheet for further analysis. When necessary, this immediate response allows you to stop and reteach to focus on the explanation. This is beneficial for students, because they receive immediate feedback and can know what they comprehend well and what they need to review.

As with interactive whiteboards, there are many lessons that are available through software and programs—and the assessments are easy to create and share. Student response systems can truly transform the way you instruct and improve the level of comprehension of students in every subject area.

References

Aarnoutse, C., Brand-Gruwel, S., & Oduber, R. (1997). Improving reading comprehension strategies through listening. *Educational Studies, 23*(2), 209–227. doi:10.1080/0305569970230205

Agnew, M.L. (2000). DRAW: A motivational reading comprehension strategy for disaffected readers. *Journal of Adolescent & Adult Literacy, 43*(6), 574–575.

Alvermann, D.E., Young, J.P., Weaver, D., Hinchman, K.A., Moore, D.W., Phelps, S.F., et al. (1996). Middle and high school students' perceptions of how they experience text-based discussions: A multicase study. *Reading Research Quarterly, 31*(3), 244–267. doi:10.1598/RRQ.31.3.2

Aronson, E., & Patnoe, S. (1997). *The jigsaw classroom: Building cooperation in the classroom* (2nd ed.). Thousand Oaks, CA: Sage.

Arreaga-Mayer, C. (1998). Increasing active student responding and improving academic performance through classwide peer tutoring. *Intervention in School and Clinic, 34*(2), 89–94. doi:10.1177/105345129803400204

Assaf, L. & Garza, R. (2007). Making magazine covers that visually count: Learning to summarize with technology. *The Reading Teacher, 60*(7), 678–680.

Au, K.H. (2009, October/November). Providing powerful comprehension instruction. *Reading Today, 27*(2), 17.

Banikowski, A.K., & Mehring, T.A. (1999). Strategies to enhance memory based on brain-research. *Focus on Exceptional Children, 32*(2), 1–16.

Barrentine, S.J. (1996). Engaging with reading through interactive read-alouds. *The Reading Teacher, 50*(1), 36–43.

Barron, R., (1969). The use of vocabulary as an advance organizer. In H.L. Herber & P.L. Sanders (Eds.), *Research in reading in the content areas: First year report* (pp. 29–39). Syracuse, NY: Syracuse University Reading and Language Arts Center.

Bean, R.M., & Zigmond, N. (1994). Adapted use of social studies textbooks in elementary classrooms: Views of classroom teachers. *Remedial and Special Education, 15*(4), 216–226. doi:10.1177/074193259401500403

Blachowicz, C.L.Z., & Ogle, D. (2001). *Reading comprehension: Strategies for independent learners.* New York: Guilford.

Bromley, K., & Modlo, M. (1997). Using cooperative learning to improve reading and writing in language arts. *Reading & Writing Quarterly, 13*(1), 21–35. doi:10.1080/1057356970130103

Bryant, D.P., Ugel, N., Thompson, S., & Hamff, A. (1999). Instructional strategies for content-area reading instruction. *Intervention in School and Clinic, 34*(5), 293–302. doi:10.1177/105345129903400506

Buehl, D. (1995). *Classroom strategies for interactive learning.* Madison: Wisconsin State Reading Association.

Buehl, D. (1997). Loud and clear: Reading aloud. *The Reading Room.* Retrieved February 7, 2011 from www.weac.org/news_and_publications/columns/reading_room/index.aspx

Buehl, D. (2009). *Classroom strategies for interactive learning.* (3rd ed.). Newark, DE: International Reading Association.

Bulgren, J., & Scanlon, D. (1998). Instructional routines and learning strategies that promote understanding of content area concepts. *Journal of Adolescent & Adult Literacy, 41*(4), 292–302.

Cantrell, R.J. (1997). K-W-L learning journals: A way to encourage reflection. *Journal of Adolescent & Adult Literacy, 40*(5), 392–393.

Caverly, D.C., Mandeville, T.F., & Nicholson, S.A. (1995). PLAN: A study-reading strategy for informational text. *Journal of Adolescent & Adult Literacy, 39*(3), 190–199.

Cochran, J.A. (1993). *Reading in the content areas for junior high and high school.* Boston: Allyn & Bacon.

Common Core State Standards Initiative. (2010). *Common core state standards for English language arts & literacy in history/social studies, science, and technical subjects.* Washington, DC: National Governors Association Center for Best Practices and the Council of Chief State School Officers.

Craig, M.T., & Yore, L.D. (1996). Middle school students' awareness of strategies for resolving comprehension difficulties in science reading. *Journal of Research and Development in Education, 29*(4), 226–238.

Delquadri, J.C., Greenwood, C.R., Stretton, K., & Hall, R.V. (1983). The peer tutoring spelling game: A classroom procedure for increasing opportunity to respond and spelling performance. *Education and Treatment of Children, 6*(3), 225–239.

DiPillo, M.L., & Sovchik, R. (1997). Exploring middle graders' mathematical thinking through journals. *Mathematics Teaching in the Middle School, 2*(5), 308–314.

Dole, J.A., Brown, K.J., & Woodrow, T. (1996). The effects of strategy instruction on the comprehension performance of at-risk students. *Reading Research Quarterly, 31*(1), 62–88. doi:10.1598/RRQ.31.1.4

Dole, J.A., Sloan, C., & Trathen, W. (1995). Teaching vocabulary within the context of literature. *Journal of Reading, 38*(6), 452–460.

Emery, D.W. (1996). Helping readers comprehend stories from the characters' perspectives. *The Reading Teacher, 49*(7), 534–541.

Fuchs, D., Fuchs, L.S., Mathes, P.G., & Simmons, D.C. (1997). Peer-assisted learning strategies: Making classrooms more responsive to diversity. *American Educational Research Journal, 34*(1), 174–206.

Fuentes, P. (1998). Reading comprehension in mathematics. *The Clearing House, 72*(2), 81–88. doi:10.1080/00098659809599602

Gunning, T.G. (1996). *Creating reading instruction for all children* (2nd ed.). Boston: Allyn & Bacon.

Hendrix, J.C. (1999). Connecting cooperative learning and social studies. *The Clearing House, 73*(1), 57–60. doi:10.1080/00098659909599642

Herber, H.L. (1978). *Teaching reading in content areas.* Englewood Cliffs, NJ: Prentice-Hall.

Hoffman, J.V. (1992). Critical reading/thinking across the curriculum: Using I-charts to support learning. *Language Arts, 69*(2), 121–127.

Ivey, G. (1999a). A multicase study in the middle school: Complexities among young adolescent readers. *Reading Research Quarterly, 34*(2), 172–192. doi:10.1598/RRQ.34.2.3

Ivey, G. (1999b). Reflections on teaching struggling middle school readers. *Journal of Adolescent & Adult Literacy, 42*(5), 372–381.

Jonson, K.F. (2006). *60 strategies for improving reading comprehension in grades K-8.* Thousand Oaks, CA: Corwin.

Kaplan, J. (1997). Acting up across the curriculum: Using creative dramatics to explore adolescent literature. *ALAN Review, 24*(3), 42–46.

Katims, D.S., & Harris, S. (1997). Improving the reading comprehension of middle school students in inclusive classrooms. *Journal of Adolescent & Adult Literacy, 41*(2), 116–123.

Koskinen, P.S. (1995). *Have you heard any good books lately? Encouraging shared reading at home with books and audiotapes.* Athens, GA: National Reading Research Center. (ERIC Document Reproduction Service No. ED385827)

Labbo, L.D., Eakle, A.J., & Montero, M.K. (2002, May). Digital Language Experience Approach: Using digital photographs and software as a Language Experience Approach innovation *Reading Online 5*(8). Retrieved August 30, 2010, from www.readingonline.org/electronic/elec_index.asp?HREF=labbo2/index.html

Labbo, L.D., Love, M.S., & Ryan, T. (2007). A vocabulary flood: Making words "sticky" with computer-response activities. *The Reading Teacher, 60*(6), 582–589.

Lamme, L.L., & Beckett, C. (1992). *Whole language in an elementary school library media center.* Syracuse, NY: ERIC Clearinghouse on Information Resources. (ERIC Document Reproduction Service No. ED346874)

Laverick, C. (2002). B-D-A strategy: Reinventing the wheel can be a good thing. *Journal of Adolescent & Adult Literacy, 46*(2), 144–147.

Leu, D.J. (2000). Literacy and technology: Deictic consequences for literacy education in an information age. In M.L. Kamil, P.B. Mosenthal, P.D. Pearson, & R. Barr (Eds.), *Handbook of reading research* (Vol. 3, pp. 743–770). Mahwah, NJ: Erlbaum.

Lewin, L., & Shoemaker, B.J. (1998). *Great performances: Creating classroom-based assessment tasks.* Alexandria, VA: Association for Supervision and Curriculum Development.

Liang, L.A., & Dole, J.A. (2006). Helping with teaching reading comprehension: Comprehension instructional frameworks. *The Reading Teacher, 59*(8), 742–752.

Malloy, J.A., & Gambrell, L.B. (2006). Approaching the unavoidable: Literacy instruction and the Internet. *The Reading Teacher, 59*(5), 482–484.

Manning, M. (1999a). Reading across the curriculum. *Teaching PreK-8, 29*(5), 83–85.

Manning, M. (1999b). Building reading skills in math. *Teaching PreK-8, 29*(7), 85–86.

Manzo, A.V. (1969). The ReQuest procedure. *Journal of Reading, 13*(2), 123–126.

Manzo, A.V., Manzo, U., & Albee, J.J. (2002). iREAP: Improving reading, writing, and thinking in the wired classroom. *Journal of Adolescent & Adult Literacy, 46*(1), 42–47.

Maring, G.H., Furman, G., & Blum-Anderson, J., (1985). Five cooperative learning strategies for mainstreamed youngsters in content area classrooms. *The Reading Teacher, 39*(3), 310–313.

Marcell, B, DeCleene, J, & Juettner, M.R. (2010). Caution! Hard hat area! Comprehension under construction: Cementing a foundation of comprehension strategy usage that carries over to independent practice. *The Reading Teacher, 63*(8), 687–691.

Massey, D.D., & Heafner, T.L. (2004). Promoting reading comprehension in social studies. *Journal of Adolescent & Adult Literacy, 48*(1), 26–40.

McGinley, W.J., & Denner, P.R., (1987). Story impressions: A prereading/writing activity. *Journal of Reading, 31*(3), 248–253.

McIntosh, M.E., & Draper, R.J. (1995). Applying the question-answer relationship strategy in mathematics. *Journal of Adolescent & Adult Literacy, 39*(2), 120–131.

McIntosh, M.E., & Draper, R.J. (1996). Using the question-answer relationship strategy to improve students' reading of mathematics texts. *The Clearing House, 69*(3), 154–162.

McLaughlin, E.M. (1987). QuIP: A writing strategy to improve comprehension of expository structure. *The Reading Teacher, 40*(7), 650–654.

McLaughlin, M., & Allen, M.B. (2002). *Guided comprehension: A teaching model for grades 3–8.* Newark, DE: International Reading Association.

McLaughlin, M., & Allen, M.B. (2009). *Guided comprehension in grades 3–8.* Newark, DE: International Reading Association.

Muth, K.D. (1997). Using cooperative learning to improve reading and writing in mathematical problem solving. *Reading & Writing Quarterly, 13*(1), 71–82. doi:10.1080/1057356970130106

National Institute of Child Health and Human Development. (2000). *Report of the National Reading Panel. Teaching children to read: An evidence-based assessment of the scientific research literature on reading and its implications for reading instruction.* (NIH Publication No. 00-4769). Washington, DC: U.S. Government Printing Office.

Nesbit, C.R., & Rogers, C.A. (1997). Using cooperative learning to improve reading and writing in science. *Reading & Writing Quarterly, 13*(1), 53–70. doi:10.1080/1057356970130105

Ogle, D.M. (1986). K-W-L: A teaching model that develops active reading of expository text. *The Reading Teacher, 39*(6), 564–570. doi:10.1598/RT.39.6.11

Ogle, D.M. (1994). Assessment: Helping our students see their learning. *Teaching PreK-8, 25*(2), 100–101.

Ogle, D.M. (2000). Make it visual: A picture is worth a thousand words. In M. McLaughlin and M.E. Vogt (Eds.), *Creativity and innovation in content area teaching* (pp. 55–71). Norwood, MA: Christopher-Gordon.

Opitz, M.F., & Eldridge, R.G. (2004). Remembering comprehension: Delving into the mysteries of teaching reading comprehension. *The Reading Teacher, 57*(8), 772–773.

Palincsar, A.S. (1984). The quest for meaning from expository text: A teacher-guided journey. In G. Duffy, L.R. Roehler, & J.D. Mason (Eds.), *Comprehension instruction: Perspectives and suggestions* (pp. 251–264). New York: Longman.

Pearman, C.J. (2008a, October/November). Using electronic tests to increase comprehension. *Reading Today, 26*(2), 34.

Pearman, C.J. (2008b). Independent reading of CD-ROM storybooks: Measuring comprehension with oral retellings. *The Reading Teacher, 61*(8), 594–602.

Pearson, P.D., & Johnson, D.D. (1978). *Teaching reading comprehension.* New York: Holt, Rinehart and Winston.

Radcliffe, R., Caverly, D., Hand, J., & Frank, D. (2008). Improving reading in a middle school science classroom. *Journal of Adolescent & Adult Literacy, 51*(5), 398–408.

Raphael, T.E. (1982). Question-answering strategies for children. *The Reading Teacher, 36*(2), 186–190.

Robinson, F.P. (1961). *Effective study.* New York: Harper & Row.

Salembier, G.B., (1999). SCAN and RUN: A reading comprehension strategy that works. *Journal of Adolescent & Adult Literacy, 42*(5), 386–394.

Schmar-Dobler, E. (2003). Reading on the Internet: The link between literacy and technology. *Journal of Adolescent & Adult Literacy, 47*(1), 80-86.

Schwartz, R.M, & Raphael, T.E., (1985). Concept of definition: A key to improving students' vocabulary. *The Reading Teacher, 39*(2), 198–205.

Shanahan, S., & Shanahan, T. (1997). Character perspective charting: Helping children to develop a more complete conception of story. *The Reading Teacher, 50*(8), 668–677.

Short, K.G, Harste, J.C, & Burke, C.L. (1996). *Creating classrooms for authors and inquirers.* (2nd ed.). Portsmouth, NH: Heinemann.

Slavin, R.E. (1988). Cooperative learning and student achievement. *Educational Leadership, 46*(2), 31–33.

Small, D. (1996). Navigating large bodies of text. *IBM Systems Journal, 35*(3), 514–525. doi:10.1147/sj.353.0514

Solon, C. (1980). The pyramid diagram: A college study skills tool. *Journal of Reading, 23*(7), 594–597.

Swanson, P.N., & De La Paz, S. (1998). Teaching effective comprehension strategies to students with learning and reading disabilities. *Intervention in School and Clinic, 33*(4), 209–218. doi:10.1177/105345129803300403

Tierney, R.J., & Readence, J.E. (2004). *Reading strategies and practices: A compendium.* (6th ed.). Boston: Allyn & Bacon.

Tovani, C. (2004). *Do I really have to teach reading? Content comprehension grades 6-12.* Markham, ON, Canada: Pembroke.

Vacca, R.T., & Vacca, J.L. (1989). *Content area reading* (3rd ed.). New York: HarperCollins.

Vallecorsa, A.L., & deBettencourt, L.U. (1997). Using a mapping procedure to teach reading and writing skills to middle grade students with learning disabilities. *Education & Treatment of Children, 20*(2), 173–188.

Vaughn, J.L., & Estes, T.H. (1986). *Reading and reasoning beyond the primary grades.* Boston: Allyn & Bacon.

Vaughn, S., & Klingner, J.K. (1999). Teaching reading comprehension through collaborative strategic reading. *Intervention in School and Clinic, 34*(5), 284–292. doi:10.1177/105345129903400505

Waldo, B. (1991). *Story pyramid.* In J.M. Macon, D. Bewell, & M.E. Vogt (Eds.), *Responses to literature: Grades K–8* (pp. 23–24). Newark, DE: International Reading Association.

Warren, J.S., & Flynt, S.W. (1995). Children with attention deficit disorder: Diagnosis and prescription of reading skill deficits. *Reading Improvement, 32*(2), 105–110.

Winograd, K., & Higgins, K.M. (1995). Writing, reading, and talking mathematics: One interdisciplinary possibility. *The Reading Teacher, 48*(4), 310–318.